PLANT-BASE
Comfort Soups

GARDEN *of* GRAPES.

First Edition: 2023

Published by Garden of Grapes.

Printed in USA

The recipes, techniques, and tips in this cookbook are intended for personal use only. The author and publisher are not responsible for any adverse effects or consequences resulting from the use of the recipes or suggestions in this book.

Library of Congress Cataloging-in-Publication Data:

First edition.
Includes index.

Manufactured in USA

Introduction

Ladies and gentlemen, seekers of comfort, and enthusiasts of soul-warming sustenance,

Welcome to the inviting embrace of the "Plant-Based Comfort Soups Cookbook: Soul-Warming Soups." As we embark on this culinary journey together, I extend to you a heartfelt welcome, a comforting invitation to explore the essence of this cookbook.

When the idea for this collection of soul-warming plant-based soups first simmered to life, it was born out of a simple, yet profound notion—that the comfort found in a steaming bowl of soup transcends all boundaries. Whether you're seeking solace from a blustery winter's day or a moment of respite from life's whirlwind, a well-crafted bowl of soup has the power to nourish both body and soul.

The inspiration for this cookbook comes from the shared love of the time-honored tradition of soup-making, combined with a deep commitment to plant-based living. It's a celebration of ingredients sourced from the earth, transformed into dishes that warm the heart. The intention is to prove that comfort need not come at the expense of our values, our health, or the planet. With each recipe, we endeavor to showcase that plant-based cooking can be an embodiment of comfort and flavor.

Within these pages, you'll discover a treasure trove of over 100 plant-based comfort classics. From hearty chowders that invoke memories of seaside escapes to velvety bisques that embody elegance, and from rustic broths that soothe the soul to exotic creations that transport your taste buds across borders—there's a soul-warming soup for every palate and every occasion.

You can expect to find not only recipes but also guidance on sourcing quality ingredients, tips for achieving the perfect consistency, and creative variations that encourage you to make each recipe your own. Whether you're an experienced soup maestro or a budding home cook, this cookbook is designed to be your trusted companion on a journey of culinary exploration.

As we venture forth into the world of "Plant-Based Comfort Soups," I invite you to savor the magic of these recipes, to create moments of connection and warmth at your own table, and to embrace the comfort that comes from nurturing your body with wholesome, plant-based nourishment.

So, dear readers, let us embark on this odyssey together, one simmering pot at a time, as we explore the art of crafting soul-warming soups that feed both body and soul. May your kitchens be filled with the comforting aroma of simmering pots, and may your hearts be warmed by the love shared over each bowl. To your health and culinary delight!

Thai Peanut Noodle Soup
See page, 50

Cooking Philosophy or Approach

Ladies and gentlemen, seekers of warmth and solace in a bowl, and advocates of the plant-based way of life,

Within the pages of "Plant-Based Comfort Soups Cookbook: Soul-Warming Soups," we embark on a culinary journey that transcends the boundaries of ordinary sustenance. It's not just about what we eat; it's about what we feel when we eat. We delve into the very essence of comfort, where each spoonful is a journey to the heart of contentment.

My approach to cooking and food is deeply rooted in the belief that great meals are not just about satisfying hunger but nourishing the soul. In a world that often moves at breakneck speed, we pause to celebrate the simple joy of a well-crafted soup, a symphony of flavors and textures that speak to our senses and memories.

Our recipes are crafted with mindfulness, selecting ingredients that not only deliver a delicious punch but also honor the planet and its inhabitants. Plant-based cooking is not a compromise; it's a revelation. We've harnessed the versatility of vegetables, legumes, grains, and spices to create a symphony of flavors that will make you forget you ever craved meat.

Specifically, our techniques are steeped in tradition while embracing innovation. We simmer, roast, and blend to coax out the deepest flavors, whether in a classic tomato bisque or a contemporary Thai-inspired coconut curry. The alchemy of spices is our secret weapon, turning a humble pot of soup into a fragrant and memorable experience.

Our ingredients are carefully selected to be readily available, ensuring that these soul-warming soups can grace your table whenever the craving strikes. We believe in the power of accessibility—food that's not only good for you but also good for your everyday life.

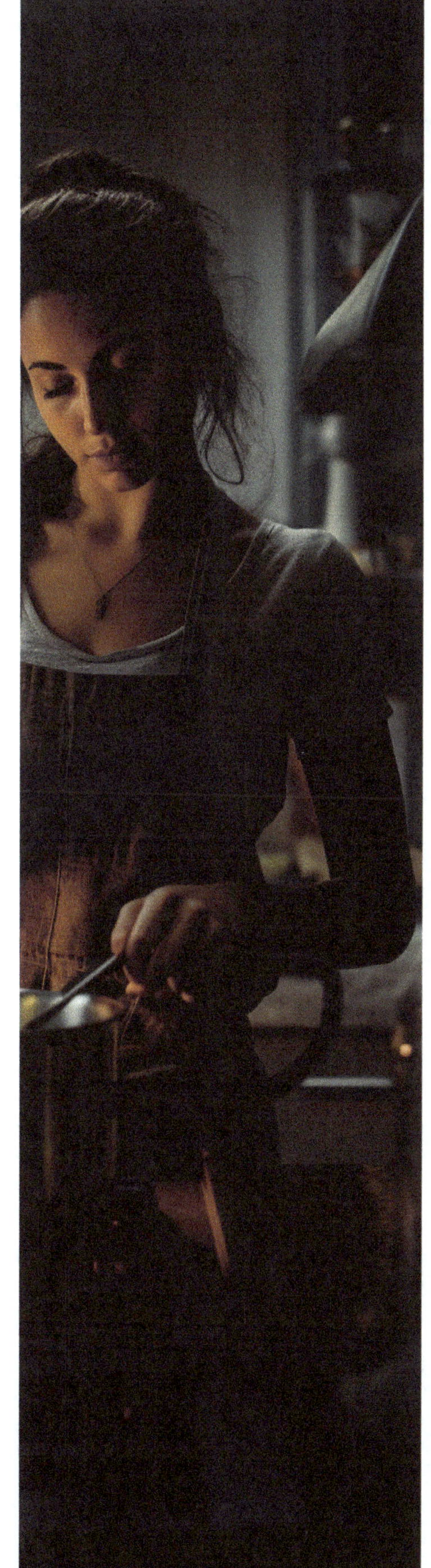

So, as you embark on this gastronomic journey through "Plant-Based Comfort Soups," remember that every simmering pot is a testament to the nourishing power of plants and the comfort they bring. It's not just about what you eat; it's about how it makes you feel. May every spoonful be a soothing embrace, a taste of comfort, and a reminder that sometimes, the simplest pleasures are the most profound. To your health and the joy of a well-warmed heart!

Vegan French Onion Soup
See page, 30

Tips for Successful Cooking

Ladies and gentlemen, seekers of comfort and champions of plant-based goodness,

Before you embark on your journey through the heartwarming pages of "Plant-Based Comfort Soups Cookbook: Soul-Warming Soups - Dive into 100+ Plant-Based Comfort Classics," I want to share some kitchen wisdom that will serve as your trusty compass in the world of soul-soothing soups.

1. Freshness is the Key: When it comes to ingredients, freshness is paramount. Seek out the ripest vegetables, the most fragrant herbs, and the finest quality spices. The quality of your ingredients will shine through in the final creation.

2. The Holy Trinity - Mirepoix: In many of our beloved comfort soup recipes, you'll encounter the classic trio of onions, carrots, and celery, known as mirepoix. Mastering the balance of these humble ingredients is the secret to a robust soup base.

3. Layer Your Flavors: Building layers of flavor is an art form. Start by sautéing your aromatics (onions, garlic, ginger) gently until they release their fragrances. Then, add spices and herbs to infuse the base with depth and character.

4. Broths and Stocks: Homemade vegetable broth is a treasure, but if time is of the essence, a good-quality store-bought option can be your ally. Remember to choose low-sodium varieties to have better control over the salt content.

5. The Simmering Symphony: Soups thrive on patience. Allow them to simmer gently, coaxing the flavors to meld together. Rushing this step is akin to skipping the crescendo of a beautiful symphony.

6. Season with Caution: Seasoning is a delicate dance. Start conservatively with salt and pepper, tasting as you go. Remember, it's easier to add more salt than to remedy an overly salty broth.

7. Texture Matters: The beauty of soups lies in their variety of textures. Blend some, leave others chunky, and always consider adding a handful of freshly chopped herbs or a drizzle of olive oil just before serving for that final touch of finesse.

8. Leftovers are a Blessing: Soups often taste even better the next day. Don't hesitate to make a large batch and savor the comforting flavors over time.

9. Personalize and Experiment: These recipes are your canvas. Don't be afraid to personalize them. Add your favorite vegetables, swap out ingredients to suit your dietary preferences, and make each bowl uniquely yours.

10. Share the Love: Few things warm the heart like a bowl of homemade soup shared with loved ones. Whip up a batch, invite friends and family to gather, and create lasting memories around the dining table.

As you embark on this culinary adventure, armed with these tips and techniques, may your journey through "Plant-Based Comfort Soups Cookbook" be filled with warmth, comfort, and the joy of savoring plant-based classics that nourish both body and soul. Happy cooking!

Vegan Taco Soup
See page, 46

Kitchen Essentials

Alright, my fellow soup enthusiasts, before we dive headfirst into the comforting world of "Plant-Based Comfort Soups Cookbook: Soul-Warming Soups," let's talk about the unsung heroes of our culinary escapades—the essential kitchen tools and equipment that will make your soup-making journey as smooth as a velvety bisque.

In the realm of hearty soups, having the right tools at your disposal is like having the perfect stock simmering on the stove; it's absolutely essential. So, let's break it down, shall we?

1. Soup Pot or Dutch Oven: This trusty workhorse will be your go-to for simmering those savory broths and stews. Go for one with a heavy bottom for even heat distribution.

2. Immersion Blender: Say goodbye to messy transfers and hello to silky-smooth soups. An immersion blender allows you to puree right in the pot.

3. Ladle: A good ladle is your serving sidekick, making it easy to portion out your liquid masterpieces.

4. Chef's Knife: A sharp chef's knife is your best friend when it comes to chopping vegetables, herbs, and more. Keep it honed for safety and precision.

5. Cutting Board: A sturdy, non-slip cutting board is essential for safe and efficient prep work.

6. Wooden Spoon: Stirring, tasting, and scooping—your trusty wooden spoon will do it all, without scratching your pots.

7. Measuring Cups and Spoons: Precision is key in cooking, so make sure you have a good set of both dry and liquid measuring cups and spoons.

8. Stockpot: For those big batches and hearty soups that'll feed a crowd, a stockpot is a must.

9. Strainer or Sieve: Perfect for removing solids from broths or straining soups for a silky finish.

10. Peeler: When your soup calls for potatoes or other veggies with skins, a reliable peeler will save you time and effort.

11. Timer: Don't rely on your memory when simmering soups. Use a timer to avoid overcooking.

12. Thermometer: For precise temperature control, especially when dealing with delicate ingredients like cream.

13. Food Processor: When you need to finely chop or blend in larger quantities, a food processor is your kitchen assistant.

14. Whisk: Perfect for mixing in those flour or cornstarch slurries to thicken your soups to perfection.

Now that you're equipped with the essential tools of the trade, let's embark on our journey through the pages of this cookbook, where we'll whip up soul-warming soups that will leave you craving seconds and thirds. Remember, these tools aren't just objects; they're your trusted allies in your quest for soup greatness. Use them wisely, and you'll be well on your way to becoming a soup maestro. Happy cooking, my fellow soup aficionados!

Flavor Pairing Suggestions

Ladies and gentlemen, as we bask in the warmth of soul-warming plant-based comfort soups from the pages of the "Plant-Based Comfort Soups Cookbook," I can't help but share a little secret with you all—flavors are like musical notes, and the kitchen is our stage. Just as a masterful symphony comes to life when notes harmonize and dance together, so does a remarkable soup when flavors pair in perfect union.

In this section, we're diving into the realm of flavor pairing suggestions—your passport to culinary creativity. Here, we'll explore ideas for complementary flavors and ingredients that not only work well together but can also serve as your guiding stars to craft your very own comforting soup creations. After all, the joy of cooking lies in the art of experimentation.

1. Tomato and Basil: Ah, the classic duo. The rich acidity of tomatoes finds its perfect counterpart in the fresh, aromatic embrace of basil. Try blending them into a velvety tomato bisque or simmer them together for a rustic tomato-basil soup that's both timeless and delightful.

2. Mushroom and Thyme: Earthy mushrooms and the warm, woody notes of thyme are a match made in soup heaven. Whether you're crafting a creamy mushroom bisque or a hearty mushroom and barley stew, this pairing adds depth and character.

3. Carrot and Ginger: The sweet, earthy crunch of carrots finds zesty companionship in the gentle heat of ginger. A carrot and ginger soup is not only vibrant in color but also an invigorating fusion of flavors.

4. Butternut Squash and Sage: Velvety butternut squash meets the savory, herbaceous charm of sage. Roast the squash, add some sautéed sage, and let your taste buds savor the symphony of autumn in a bowl.

5. Lentil and Cumin: Nutty lentils and the warm, smoky essence of cumin are a marriage made for hearty soups. Try this pairing in a nourishing lentil and cumin soup that's both protein-packed and bursting with flavor.

6. Potato and Chive: Creamy potatoes and the mild, oniony allure of chives create a delightful harmony. A potato and chive soup is the epitome of comfort on a chilly evening.

7. Spinach and Nutmeg: Leafy spinach and the subtle, sweet spice of nutmeg come together elegantly. Experiment with this pairing in a creamy spinach and nutmeg soup that's both elegant and soothing.

8. Coconut and Lemongrass: Creamy coconut milk and the zesty, citrusy notes of lemongrass transport your taste buds to the tropics. A coconut and lemongrass-infused soup is a delightful departure from the ordinary.

Remember, my fellow culinary adventurers, these are just a few guiding stars in the constellation of flavors. Feel free to mix and match, improvise, and let your creativity flow. In the world of plant-based comfort soups, the possibilities are as endless as the joy they bring. So, grab your ladle and compose your flavor symphony—one comforting bowl at a time. Bon appétit!

INDEX

Chapter 1: Cozy Breakfast Soups, 1
Creamy Vegan Oatmeal Porridge, 2
Spiced Pumpkin Breakfast Soup, 3
Quinoa and Berry Breakfast Soup, 4
Apple Cinnamon Breakfast Soup, 5
Sweet Potato and Coconut Breakfast Soup, 6
Chia Pudding Breakfast Soup, 7
Peanut Butter Banana Breakfast Soup, 8
Gingerbread Breakfast Soup, 9
Blueberry Almond Breakfast Soup, 10
Chapter 2: Hearty Lunchtime Favorites, 11
Classic Minestrone Soup, 12
Roasted Red Pepper and Tomato Bisque, 13
Lentil and Vegetable Soup, 14
Mushroom Barley Soup, 15
Thai Coconut Curry Soup, 16
Vegan Potato Leek Soup, 17
Creamy Broccoli Cheddar Soup, 18
Moroccan Chickpea Stew, 19
Vegan Pho Soup, 20
Tuscan White Bean Soup, 21
Chapter 3: Comforting Dinner Delights, 22
Butternut Squash Soup with Sage, 23
Vegan Chili, 24
Creamy Tomato Basil Soup, 25
Sweet Potato and Black Bean Soup, 26
Vegan Corn Chowder, 27
Chickpea and Spinach Soup, 28
Creamy Wild Mushroom Soup, 29
Vegan French Onion Soup, 30
Roasted Vegetable and Quinoa Soup, 31
Vegan Ramen Soup, 32
Chapter 4: Nutrient-Rich Breakfast Soups, 33
Green Goddess Breakfast Soup, 34
Spinach and Kale Breakfast Soup, 35
Blueberry Avocado Breakfast Soup, 36
Turmeric Ginger Breakfast Soup, 37
Mango Coconut Breakfast Soup, 38
Berry Chia Breakfast Soup, 39
Almond Joy Breakfast Soup, 40

Papaya and Lime Breakfast Soup, 41
Peanut Butter Banana Breakfast Soup, 42
Raspberry Almond Breakfast Soup, 43
Chapter 5: Wholesome Lunchtime Bowls, 45
Vegan Taco Soup, 46
Italian Minestrone Soup, 47
Vegan Gumbo, 48
Spinach and Lentil Soup, 49
Thai Peanut Noodle Soup, 50
Vegan Borscht Soup, 51
Mexican Tortilla Soup, 52
Vegan Soba Noodle Soup, 53
Mediterranean Chickpea Soup, 54
Vegan Eggplant Parmesan Soup, 55
Chapter 6: Satisfying Dinner Comforts, 56
Vegan Cream of Mushroom Soup, 57
Vegan Lasagna Soup, 58
Vegan Jambalaya, 59
Vegan Creamy Potato Soup, 60
Vegan Shepherd's Pie Soup, 61
Vegan Cabbage Soup, 62
Vegan Egg Drop Soup, 63
Vegan Tortilla Pie Soup, 64
Vegan Tomato and Basil Risotto Soup, 65
Vegan Mushroom Stroganoff Soup, 66
Chapter 7: Energizing Breakfast Bowls, 67
Acai Bowl, 68
Dragon Fruit Smoothie Bowl, 69
Chocolate Peanut Butter Breakfast Soup, 70
Mango Turmeric Breakfast Soup, 71
Strawberry Banana Breakfast Soup, 72
Avocado and Spinach Breakfast Soup, 73
Kiwi and Pineapple Breakfast Soup, 74
Cherry Almond Breakfast Soup, 75
Peach Cobbler Breakfast Soup, 76
Raspberry Chia Breakfast Soup, 77
Chapter 8: Flavorful Lunchtime Classics, 78
Vegan Clam Chowder, 79
Vegan Goulash Soup, 80
Vegan Tomato Rice Soup, 81
Vegan Thai Green Curry Soup, 82
Vegan Sweet Potato Bisque, 83
Vegan Roasted Garlic Soup, 84

Vegan Pumpkin and Sage Soup, 85
Vegan Spinach and Artichoke Soup, 86
Vegan Corn and Potato Chowder, 87
Vegan Lentil and Kale Soup, 88
Chapter 9: Cozy Dinner Soups, 89
Vegan Creamy Asparagus Soup, 90
Vegan Stuffed Bell Pepper Soup, 91
Vegan Cajun Red Beans and Rice Soup, 92
Vegan Ratatouille Soup, 93
Vegan Creamy Pesto Zucchini Soup, 94
Vegan Korean Kimchi Soup, 95
Vegan Cuban Black Bean Soup, 96
Vegan Thai Basil Eggplant Soup, 97
Vegan Mushroom and Spinach Tortellini Soup, 98
Vegan Alfredo Pasta Soup, 99
Chapter 10: Nourishing Breakfast Starters, 100
Vegan Breakfast Burrito Soup, 101
Vegan Blueberry Pancake Soup, 102
Vegan Breakfast Enchilada Soup, 103
Vegan Breakfast Quesadilla Soup, 104
Vegan Tofu Scramble Soup, 105
Vegan Breakfast Tacos Soup, 106
Vegan Breakfast Sandwich Soup, 107
Vegan Breakfast Hash Soup, 108
Vegan Breakfast Pizza Soup, 109
Vegan Breakfast Wrap Soup, 110
Chapter 11: Revitalizing Breakfast Soups, 111
Vegan Blueberry Muffin Soup, 112
Vegan Breakfast BLT Soup, 113
Vegan Breakfast Bowl Soup, 114
Vegan Breakfast Sushi Soup, 115
Vegan Breakfast Bruschetta Soup, 116
Vegan Breakfast Nachos Soup, 117
Vegan Breakfast Bagel Soup, 118
Vegan Breakfast Samosa Soup, 119
Vegan Breakfast Spring Rolls Soup, 120
Vegan Breakfast Empanadas Soup, 121

Chapter 1:
Cozy Breakfast Soups

2 servings | 250 | 15 min

A cozy, plant-based breakfast classic.

Creamy Vegan Oatmeal Porridge

Ingredients:

- 1 cup rolled oats
- 2 cups almond milk
- 2 tbsp maple syrup
- 1 tsp vanilla extract
- Pinch of salt
- Optional toppings: berries, nuts, and seeds

Directions

1. In a saucepan, combine oats, almond milk, maple syrup, vanilla, and a pinch of salt. Simmer over low heat, stirring until creamy (about 10 minutes).
2. Serve hot, topped with your favorite berries, nuts, and seeds.

4 servings 180 20 min

Spiced Pumpkin Breakfast Soup

A fall-inspired breakfast delight with a twist.

Ingredients:

- 2 cups canned pumpkin puree
- 3 cups vegetable broth
- 1 tsp ground cinnamon
- 1/2 tsp ground nutmeg
- 1/4 tsp ground cloves
- 1/4 cup coconut milk

Directions

1. In a pot, combine pumpkin puree, vegetable broth, and spices. Simmer for 15 minutes.
2. Stir in coconut milk and heat for 5 more minutes.
3. Serve warm.

Substitutions

- Use butternut squash puree instead of pumpkin puree if desired.

2 servings

320

25 min

A protein-packed breakfast with a fruity twist.

Quinoa and Berry Breakfast Soup

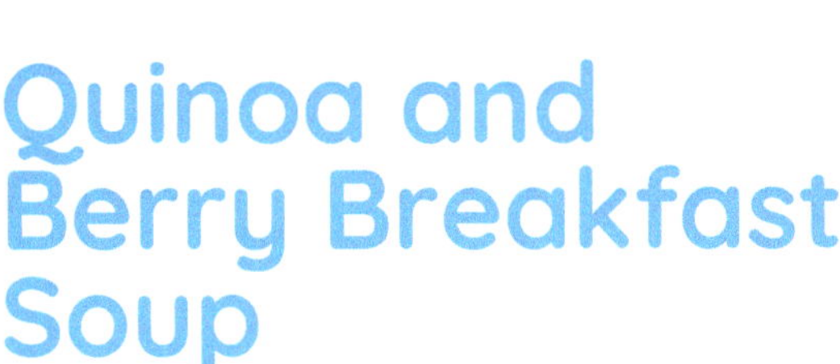

Ingredients:

- 1/2 cup quinoa
- 1 cup almond milk
- 1 cup mixed berries
- 2 tbsp honey
- 1/2 tsp vanilla extract
- Pinch of salt

Directions

1. Rinse quinoa and cook in almond milk until tender (about 15 minutes).
2. Stir in berries, honey, vanilla, and a pinch of salt.
3. Serve warm.

Substitutions

- Use any sweetener you prefer.

4 servings | 220 | 15 min

Apple Cinnamon Breakfast Soup

Easy

A comforting blend of apples and spices.

Ingredients:

- 4 apples, peeled and chopped
- 4 cups water
- 1/2 tsp ground cinnamon
- 2 tbsp maple syrup
- 1/2 cup rolled oats

Directions

1. In a pot, simmer apples in water until soft (about 10 minutes).
2. Blend until smooth.
3. Stir in cinnamon, maple syrup, and oats.
4. Serve hot.

Substitutions

- Adjust sweetness to taste.

3 servings   280   30 min

Creamy and satisfying, with a tropical twist.

Sweet Potato and Coconut Breakfast Soup

Ingredients:

- 2 sweet potatoes, peeled and diced
- 2 cups coconut milk
- 1 tsp curry powder
- 1/4 tsp cayenne pepper
- Salt and pepper to taste

Directions

1. Boil sweet potatoes until tender (about 15 minutes).
2. Blend with coconut milk, curry powder, cayenne, salt, and pepper until smooth.
3. Reheat and serve.

Substitutions

- Use pumpkin for a variation.

2 servings   180   5 min

Chia Pudding Breakfast Soup

A quick and nutritious breakfast in a bowl.

Ingredients:

- 1/4 cup chia seeds
- 1.5 cups almond milk
- 2 tbsp honey
- 1/2 tsp vanilla extract
- Fresh fruit for topping

Directions

1. Mix chia seeds, almond milk, honey, and vanilla. Refrigerate for at least 2 hours (or overnight).
2. Top with fresh fruit before serving.

Substitutions

- Use agave nectar for a vegan option.

2 servings | **300** | **10 min**

Peanut Butter Banana Breakfast Soup

A creamy blend of nutty and fruity goodness.

Ingredients:

- 2 ripe bananas
- 2 cups almond milk
- 2 tbsp peanut butter
- 1 tbsp honey
- 1/2 tsp cinnamon
- 1/4 cup granola

Directions

1. Blend bananas, almond milk, peanut butter, honey, and cinnamon until smooth.
2. Pour into bowls and top with granola.
3. Enjoy!

Substitutions

- Use any nut butter of your choice.

4 servings | 260 | 20 min

Gingerbread Breakfast Soup

A warm and spiced morning delight.

Ingredients:

- 2 cups oat milk
- 1/2 cup molasses
- 2 tsp gingerbread spice mix
- 1/2 cup steel-cut oats
- 1/4 cup raisins

Directions

1. In a pot, heat oat milk and molasses until hot but not boiling.
2. Stir in gingerbread spice and oats.
3. Cook until oats are tender.
4. Add raisins and serve.

Substitutions

- Adjust spice level to taste.

2 servings | 280 | 15 min

Blueberry Almond Breakfast Soup

A fruity and nutty way to start your day.

Ingredients:

- 1 cup blueberries (fresh or frozen)
- 1/2 cup almond butter
- 2 cups almond milk
- 2 tbsp honey
- 1/2 tsp almond extract

Directions

1. Blend blueberries, almond butter, almond milk, honey, and almond extract until smooth.
2. Heat gently if desired.
3. Sip and enjoy!

Substitutions

- Use other nut butter as a substitute.

Chapter 2:
Hearty Lunchtime Favorites

4 servings | 220 | 30 min

Classic Minestrone Soup

A timeless Italian soup with a medley of flavors.

Ingredients:

- 1 cup diced onions
- 1/2 cup diced carrots
- 1/2 cup diced celery
- 1 cup diced zucchini
- 1 cup canned diced tomatoes
- 1 cup cooked kidney beans
- 4 cups vegetable broth
- 1 cup small pasta
- 1 tsp dried Italian herbs

Directions

1. In a pot, sauté onions, carrots, and celery until soft.
2. Add zucchini, tomatoes, kidney beans, vegetable broth, pasta, and herbs.
3. Simmer until pasta is tender.
4. Serve hot.

Substitutions

- Use any preferred pasta.
- Add spinach for extra greens.

4 servings **180** **40 min**

Roasted Red Pepper and Tomato Bisque

A velvety, smoky blend of roasted peppers and tomatoes.

Ingredients:

- 4 red bell peppers
- 4 tomatoes
- 1 onion, chopped
- 2 cloves garlic, minced
- 4 cups vegetable broth
- 1/2 cup coconut milk
- Salt and pepper to taste

Directions

1. Roast peppers and tomatoes until charred.
2. Sauté onion and garlic until fragrant.
3. Blend peppers, tomatoes, onion, garlic, broth, and coconut milk until smooth.
4. Reheat and season to taste.
5. Enjoy!

Substitutions

- Use almond milk for a lighter option.
- Add a dash of paprika for extra smokiness.

4 servings | 250 | 35 min

Lentil and Vegetable Soup

Hearty and nutritious, perfect for a satisfying meal.

Ingredients:

- 1 cup dried green lentils
- 1 onion, chopped
- 2 carrots, chopped
- 2 celery stalks, chopped
- 2 cloves garlic, minced
- 1 tsp ground cumin
- 1 tsp paprika
- 6 cups vegetable broth

Directions

1. Rinse lentils and cook until tender.
2. Sauté onion, carrots, celery, and garlic until soft.
3. Add cooked lentils, cumin, paprika, and vegetable broth.
4. Simmer for 20 minutes.
5. Serve hot.

Substitutions

- Add spinach or kale for extra greens.
- Adjust spices to taste.

4 servings | 280 | 45 min

Normal

Mushroom Barley Soup

Earthy mushrooms and hearty barley in a warm embrace.

Ingredients:

- 2 cups sliced mushrooms
- 1 onion, chopped
- 2 carrots, chopped
- 2 celery stalks, chopped
- 1 cup pearl barley
- 8 cups vegetable broth
- 1 tsp dried thyme
- Salt and pepper to taste

Directions

1. Sauté mushrooms, onion, carrots, and celery until soft.
2. Add barley, vegetable broth, thyme, salt, and pepper.
3. Simmer for 30 minutes until barley is tender.
4. Enjoy!

Substitutions

- Use wild mushrooms for a richer flavor.
- Add a splash of white wine for extra depth.

4 servings | 350 | 40 min

Thai Coconut Curry Soup

A vibrant and aromatic Thai-inspired soup.

Ingredients:

- 1 cup sliced bell peppers
- 1 cup sliced carrots
- 1 cup sliced mushrooms
- 1 cup coconut milk
- 4 cups vegetable broth
- 2 tbsp red curry paste
- 1 tbsp soy sauce
- 1 tbsp brown sugar
- 1 cup rice noodles
- Fresh cilantro for garnish

Directions

1. Sauté bell peppers, carrots, and mushrooms until tender.
2. Add coconut milk, vegetable broth, red curry paste, soy sauce, and sugar.
3. Simmer for 20 minutes.
4. Cook rice noodles separately.
5. Serve soup over noodles, garnished with cilantro.
6. Delight in the flavors!

Substitutions

- Adjust curry paste for preferred spice level.
- Add tofu for extra protein.

4 servings   260   30 min

Vegan Potato Leek Soup

Creamy and comforting, a classic favorite.

Ingredients:

- 4 potatoes, peeled and diced
- 2 leeks, sliced
- 1 onion, chopped
- 2 cloves garlic, minced
- 4 cups vegetable broth
- 1 cup almond milk
- Salt and pepper to taste

Directions

1. Sauté leeks, onion, and garlic until soft.
2. Add potatoes, vegetable broth, and almond milk.
3. Simmer until potatoes are tender.
4. Blend until creamy.
5. Season to taste.
6. Enjoy the warmth!

Substitutions

- Use cashew milk for extra creaminess.
- Add fresh herbs for a twist.

4 servings | 320 | 35 min

Creamy Broccoli Cheddar Soup

A cheesy indulgence with the goodness of broccoli.

Ingredients:

- 2 cups chopped broccoli
- 1 onion, chopped
- 2 cloves garlic, minced
- 4 cups vegetable broth
- 2 cups shredded cheddar cheese
- 1 cup milk
- Salt and pepper to taste

Directions

1. Sauté broccoli, onion, and garlic until tender.
2. Add vegetable broth and simmer until broccoli is soft.
3. Blend until smooth.
4. Stir in cheddar cheese, milk, salt, and pepper.
5. Reheat and serve.
6. Savor the cheesy goodness!

Substitutions

- Use vegan cheese for a dairy-free option.
- Add a pinch of nutmeg for extra flavor.

4 servings   280   40 min

Moroccan Chickpea Stew

Exotic flavors of North Africa in a hearty stew.

Ingredients:

- 2 cups cooked chickpeas
- 1 onion, chopped
- 2 carrots, chopped
- 2 cloves garlic, minced
- 1 tsp ground cumin
- 1 tsp ground coriander
- 1/2 tsp cinnamon
- 1 can diced tomatoes
- 4 cups vegetable broth

Directions

1. Sauté onion, carrots, and garlic until soft.
2. Add chickpeas, spices, tomatoes, and vegetable broth.
3. Simmer for 20 minutes.
4. Enjoy the Moroccan magic!

Substitutions

- Add raisins for sweetness.
- Serve over couscous or quinoa.

4 servings | 230 | 45 min

Vegan Pho Soup

A Vietnamese classic with plant-based flair.

Ingredients:

- 8 cups vegetable broth
- 4 oz rice noodles
- 1 onion, sliced
- 3 cloves garlic, minced
- 2 tsp ginger, grated
- 1 cinnamon stick
- 2 star anise
- 1 cup sliced mushrooms
- Toppings: bean sprouts, lime, basil, sriracha

Directions

1. Sauté onion, garlic, and ginger until fragrant.
2. Add cinnamon, star anise, mushrooms, and vegetable broth.
3. Simmer for 30 minutes.
4. Cook rice noodles separately.
5. Serve soup over noodles with desired toppings.
6. Savor the flavors!

Substitutions

- Customize toppings to your preference.
- Adjust spice level with sriracha.

 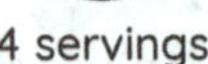  

4 servings   240   35 min

Easy

A rustic Italian soup with creamy white beans.

Tuscan White Bean Soup

Ingredients:

- 2 cans white beans, drained and rinsed
- 1 onion, chopped
- 2 carrots, chopped
- 2 celery stalks, chopped
- 2 cloves garlic, minced
- 4 cups vegetable broth
- 2 cups spinach leaves
- 1 tsp dried rosemary
- Salt and pepper to taste

Directions

1. Sauté onion, carrots, celery, and garlic until tender.
2. Add white beans, vegetable broth, spinach, rosemary, salt, and pepper.
3. Simmer for 15 minutes.
4. Enjoy the Tuscan warmth!

Substitutions

- Add a splash of balsamic vinegar for extra flavor.
- Use kale instead of spinach.

Chapter 3:
Comforting Dinner Delights

4 servings   220   40 min

Butternut Squash Soup with Sage

Normal

A velvety, autumn-inspired soup with a touch of sage.

Ingredients:

- 1 butternut squash, peeled and cubed
- 1 onion, chopped
- 2 cloves garlic, minced
- 4 cups vegetable broth
- 1/2 cup coconut milk
- 1 tsp dried sage
- Salt and pepper to taste

Directions

1. Roast butternut squash until tender (about 25 minutes).
2. Sauté onion and garlic until fragrant.
3. Blend squash, onion, garlic, vegetable broth, coconut milk, sage, salt, and pepper until smooth.
4. Reheat and enjoy!

Substitutions

- Use thyme or rosemary for a different herb flavor.
- Swap coconut milk for almond milk for a lighter version.

4 servings   **300**   **45 min**

Vegan Chili

A hearty and spicy chili loaded with plant-based goodness.

Ingredients:

- 2 cups cooked kidney beans
- 2 cups cooked black beans
- 1 onion, chopped
- 2 cloves garlic, minced
- 1 bell pepper, chopped
- 1 can diced tomatoes
- 2 cups vegetable broth
- 2 tbsp chili powder
- 1 tsp cumin
- Salt and pepper to taste

Directions

1. Sauté onion, garlic, and bell pepper until soft.
2. Add beans, tomatoes, vegetable broth, chili powder, cumin, salt, and pepper.
3. Simmer for 30 minutes.
4. Dig in!

Substitutions

- Customize spice level with more or less chili powder.
- Add corn or quinoa for extra texture.

4 servings | 240 | 35 min

Creamy Tomato Basil Soup

A classic favorite with a creamy, tomatoey twist.

Ingredients:

- 4 cups canned tomatoes
- 1 onion, chopped
- 2 cloves garlic, minced
- 1/2 cup coconut milk
- 1 tsp dried basil
- Salt and pepper to taste

Directions

1. Sauté onion and garlic until fragrant.
2. Add canned tomatoes, coconut milk, basil, salt, and pepper.
3. Simmer for 20 minutes.
4. Blend until creamy.
5. Enjoy with a sprinkle of fresh basil!

Substitutions

- Use almond milk for a lighter version.
- Add a pinch of red pepper flakes for heat.

4 servings | 280 | 40 min

Sweet Potato and Black Bean Soup

A sweet and savory blend of sweet potatoes and black beans.

Ingredients:

- 2 sweet potatoes, peeled and diced
- 1 onion, chopped
- 2 cloves garlic, minced
- 2 cups cooked black beans
- 4 cups vegetable broth
- 1 tsp ground cumin
- 1 tsp smoked paprika
- Salt and pepper to taste

Directions

1. Sauté sweet potatoes, onion, and garlic until tender.
2. Add black beans, vegetable broth, cumin, paprika, salt, and pepper.
3. Simmer for 30 minutes.
4. Savor the sweetness!

Substitutions

- Adjust spices to taste.
- Add kale or spinach for greens.

4 servings

260

30 min

Vegan Corn Chowder

A creamy and corny delight with a vegan twist.

Ingredients:

- 4 cups corn kernels (fresh or frozen)
- 1 onion, chopped
- 2 cloves garlic, minced
- 4 cups vegetable broth
- 1 cup coconut milk
- 2 tbsp nutritional yeast
- Salt and pepper to taste

Directions

1. Sauté onion and garlic until fragrant.
2. Add corn, vegetable broth, coconut milk, nutritional yeast, salt, and pepper.
3. Simmer for 15 minutes.
4. Dive into the creamy goodness!

Substitutions

- Use almond milk for a lighter version.
- Add diced potatoes for extra heartiness.

4 servings   220   25 min

Chickpea and Spinach Soup

A simple and nutritious soup with the goodness of chickpeas.

Ingredients:

- 2 cans chickpeas, drained and rinsed
- 1 onion, chopped
- 2 cloves garlic, minced
- 4 cups vegetable broth
- 4 cups fresh spinach
- 1 tsp ground turmeric
- Salt and pepper to taste

Directions

1. Sauté onion and garlic until fragrant.
2. Add chickpeas, vegetable broth, turmeric, salt, and pepper.
3. Simmer for 10 minutes.
4. Stir in fresh spinach and let wilt.
5. Enjoy the simplicity!

Substitutions

- Customize greens with kale or Swiss chard.
- Add lemon juice for a citrusy twist.

4 servings | 290 | 40 min

Creamy Wild Mushroom Soup

An indulgent mushroom medley in a velvety soup.

Ingredients:

- 2 cups assorted wild mushrooms, sliced
- 1 onion, chopped
- 2 cloves garlic, minced
- 4 cups vegetable broth
- 1/2 cup cashew cream
- 1 tsp thyme
- Salt and pepper to taste

Directions

1. Sauté mushrooms, onion, and garlic until tender.
2. Add vegetable broth, cashew cream, thyme, salt, and pepper.
3. Simmer for 20 minutes.
4. Relish the mushroom richness!

Substitutions

- Use almond cream for a lighter version.
- Add a dash of truffle oil for extra luxury.

4 servings

230

50 min

Vegan French Onion Soup

A vegan twist on the classic French onion soup.

Ingredients:

- 4 onions, thinly sliced
- 2 cloves garlic, minced
- 4 cups vegetable broth
- 1 tsp soy sauce
- 1 tsp balsamic vinegar
- 4 slices vegan bread
- 1 cup vegan cheese, shredded
- Salt and pepper to taste

Directions

1. Sauté onions and garlic until caramelized.
2. Add vegetable broth, soy sauce, and balsamic vinegar.
3. Simmer for 30 minutes.
4. Toast bread and top with vegan cheese.
5. Broil until cheese is melted and bubbly.
6. Float cheesy bread on soup and enjoy!

Substitutions

- Customize cheese and bread to your preference.
- Add a splash of red wine for depth.

 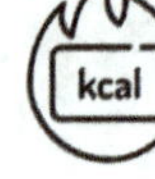 

4 servings   310   45 min

Roasted Vegetable and Quinoa Soup

A wholesome soup with roasted veggies and protein-packed quinoa.

Ingredients:

- 2 cups mixed roasted vegetables
(bell peppers, zucchini, carrots, etc.)
- 1 onion, chopped
- 2 cloves garlic, minced
- 1 cup quinoa
- 4 cups vegetable broth
- 1 tsp dried thyme
- Salt and pepper to taste

Directions

1. Sauté onion and garlic until fragrant.
2. Add roasted vegetables, quinoa, vegetable broth, thyme, salt, and pepper.
3. Simmer for 20 minutes until quinoa is cooked.
4. Enjoy the heartiness!

Substitutions

- Use your favorite roasted veggies.
- Add kale or spinach for extra greens.

4 servings   320   35 min

Vegan Ramen Soup

A Japanese-inspired ramen with a vegan twist.

Ingredients:

- 8 cups vegetable broth
- 8 oz ramen noodles
- 1 cup sliced mushrooms
- 1 cup sliced bok choy
- 1 cup sliced tofu
- 2 tbsp soy sauce
- 1 tsp sesame oil
- Green onions and nori for garnish

Directions

1. Cook ramen noodles separately according to package instructions.
2. In a pot, bring vegetable broth to a simmer.
3. Add mushrooms, bok choy, tofu, soy sauce, and sesame oil.
4. Simmer for 10 minutes.
5. Serve over cooked ramen noodles.
6. Garnish with green onions and nori.
7. Enjoy your vegan ramen!

Substitutions

- Customize toppings with your favorite veggies and herbs.
- Adjust soy sauce for preferred saltiness.

Chapter 4:
Nutrient-Rich Breakfast Soups

2 servings   220   15 min

Green Goddess Breakfast Soup

A vibrant green soup packed with nutrients.

Ingredients:

- 2 cups baby spinach
- 1 avocado
- 1 cucumber, peeled and chopped
- 1 cup coconut water
- Juice of 1 lime
- 2 tbsp fresh basil leaves
- Salt and pepper to taste

Directions

1. Blend spinach, avocado, cucumber, coconut water, lime juice, and basil until smooth.
2. Season with salt and pepper to taste.
3. Serve chilled.

2 servings | 230 | 20 min

Spinach and Kale Breakfast Soup

A power-packed soup with leafy greens.

Ingredients:

- 2 cups spinach
- 1 cup kale
- 1 small potato, peeled and diced
- 1 cup vegetable broth
- 1/2 cup almond milk
- 1/4 tsp nutmeg
- Salt and pepper to taste

Directions

1. Boil potato in vegetable broth until tender (about 10 minutes).
2. Add spinach and kale, and simmer for 5 more minutes.
3. Blend with almond milk and nutmeg until smooth.
4. Season to taste and enjoy!

Substitutions

- Use any greens you prefer.
- Substitute almond milk with your choice of milk.

2 servings | 280 | 10 min

A fruity and creamy delight.

Blueberry Avocado Breakfast Soup

Ingredients:

- 1 avocado
- 1 cup blueberries
- 1 banana
- 1 cup almond milk
- 1 tbsp honey
- 1/2 tsp vanilla extract
- Fresh blueberries for garnish

Directions

1. Blend avocado, blueberries, banana, almond milk, honey, and vanilla until smooth.
2. Pour into bowls and garnish with fresh blueberries.
3. Enjoy the fruity goodness!

Substitutions

- Use maple syrup as a vegan sweetener.
- Add chia seeds for extra texture.

2 servings   150   15 min

Turmeric Ginger Breakfast Soup

A warming and anti-inflammatory morning boost.

Ingredients:

- 2 carrots, peeled and chopped
- 1 apple, cored and chopped
- 1 tsp turmeric
- 1/2 tsp ginger
- 2 cups water
- Juice of 1 lemon
- Honey or maple syrup to taste

Directions

1. Boil carrots and apple in water until soft (about 10 minutes).
2. Blend with turmeric, ginger, and lemon juice until smooth.
3. Sweeten to taste with honey or maple syrup.
4. Sip and start your day right!

Substitutions

- Adjust sweetness to your liking.
- Add a pinch of black pepper to enhance turmeric's absorption.

2 servings   320   10 min

Mango Coconut Breakfast Soup

A tropical blend of mango and creamy coconut.

Ingredients:

- 2 ripe mangoes, peeled and chopped
- 1 cup coconut milk
- 1/2 cup Greek yogurt
- 1 tbsp honey
- 1/2 tsp vanilla extract
- Fresh mango chunks for topping

Directions

1. Blend ripe mangoes, coconut milk, Greek yogurt, honey, and vanilla extract until creamy.
2. Pour into bowls and top with fresh mango chunks.
3. Dive into the tropical goodness!

Substitutions

- Use coconut yogurt for a vegan option.
- Add shredded coconut for extra texture.

2 servings   280   15 min

Berry Chia Breakfast Soup

A nutritious blend of berries and chia seeds.

Ingredients:

- 1 cup mixed berries (strawberries, raspberries, blueberries)
- 2 tbsp chia seeds
- 1 cup almond milk
- 1 tbsp honey
- 1/2 tsp vanilla extract
- Fresh berries for garnish

Directions

1. Blend mixed berries, chia seeds, almond milk, honey, and vanilla extract until well combined.
2. Pour into bowls and garnish with fresh berries.
3. Let it sit for 10 minutes to thicken.
4. Enjoy the berry goodness!

Substitutions

- Use agave nectar for a vegan sweetener.
- Add granola for extra crunch.

2 servings | 320 | 10 min

Almond Joy Breakfast Soup

A dessert-inspired morning treat.

Ingredients:

- 1/2 cup almonds
- 2 tbsp cocoa powder
- 2 ripe bananas
- 1 cup almond milk
- 1 tbsp honey
- 1/2 tsp coconut extract
- Toasted coconut flakes for garnish

Directions

1. Blend almonds and cocoa powder until finely ground.
2. Add bananas, almond milk, honey, and coconut extract; blend until smooth.
3. Pour into bowls and garnish with toasted coconut flakes.
4. Savor the dessert-like flavors!

Substitutions

- Use maple syrup for a vegan sweetener.
- Add a pinch of sea salt for extra depth.

2 servings | 180 | 15 min

Papaya and Lime Breakfast Soup

A tropical twist with papaya and zesty lime.

Ingredients:

- 2 cups ripe papaya, peeled and chopped
- Juice of 2 limes
- 1 cup coconut water
- 1 tbsp honey
- Fresh mint leaves for garnish

Directions

1. Blend ripe papaya, lime juice, coconut water, and honey until smooth.
2. Pour into bowls and garnish with fresh mint leaves.
3. Feel the tropical vibes!

Substitutions

- Use agave nectar for a vegan sweetener.
- Add a squeeze of lemon for extra zing.

2 servings | 280 | 10 min

Peanut Butter Banana Breakfast Soup

A creamy and nutty breakfast indulgence.

Ingredients:

- 2 bananas
- 1/4 cup peanut butter
- 1 cup almond milk
- 1 tbsp honey
- 1/2 tsp vanilla extract
- Sliced bananas and chopped peanuts for topping

Directions

1. Blend bananas, peanut butter, almond milk, honey, and vanilla extract until creamy.
2. Pour into bowls and top with sliced bananas and chopped peanuts.
3. Enjoy the nutty delight!

Substitutions

- Use almond butter for a variation.
- Add a pinch of cinnamon for extra flavor.

 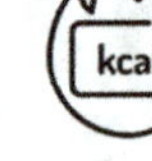 

2 servings   250   15 min

Raspberry Almond Breakfast Soup

A delightful blend of raspberries and almonds.

Ingredients:

- 1 cup raspberries
- 1/2 cup almonds
- 1 cup almond milk
- 1 tbsp honey
- 1/2 tsp almond extract
- Fresh raspberries and slivered almonds for garnish

Directions

1. Blend raspberries, almonds, almond milk, honey, and almond extract until well combined.
2. Pour into bowls and garnish with fresh raspberries and slivered almonds.
3. Relish the berry-almond fusion!

Substitutions

- Use agave nectar for a vegan sweetener.
- Add a splash of rosewater for fragrance.

We have a small favor to ask

Ladies and gentlemen, seekers of comfort and warmth in a bowl, and fellow enthusiasts of plant-based soul food,

Before we dive back into the enticing world of "Plant-Based Comfort Soups Cookbook: Soul-Warming Soups - Dive into 100+ Plant-Based Comfort Classics," I'd like to pause for a moment and have a heart-to-heart conversation.

You see, in the realm of cookbooks, reviews are the currency of culinary culture. They are the whispered secrets that guide chefs and home cooks alike to culinary treasures. Reviews, my friends, are as rare as the perfect simmer and as elusive as that one secret ingredient that elevates a dish from ordinary to extraordinary.

As a small publisher, every review is a precious gem in our culinary treasure chest. Your words have the power to inspire, to guide, and to ignite the passions of future cooks who dare to embark on this plant-based journey of warmth and comfort.

So, here's my humble request: if you've found solace and nourishment within these pages, if these plant-based comfort classics have brought you warmth on a cold day and solace in times of need, could you spare a moment?

Please, revisit the app or platform where you acquired this cookbook, and there, you'll discover a review button waiting for your input. A star rating and a brief sentence capturing your thoughts would be the culinary equivalent of a standing ovation in our world.

I promise you, every review is not just welcomed but cherished. We understand that, like in any kitchen, even the most skilled chefs may occasionally make a minor mistake. If you happen to spot any such hiccup along the way, please understand that we've poured our hearts into this cookbook. We're human, and in the world of cooking, a touch of imperfection is part of the magic.

With that, my fellow soup lovers, let's return to the recipes that warm our hearts and nourish our souls. As we simmer and savor, remember that your words have the power to bring warmth and comfort to others as they embark on their own culinary journeys. To your health, your happiness, and your next bowl of soul-warming plant-based comfort. Thank you.

Chapter 5: Wholesome Lunchtime Bowls

4 servings | 320 | 30 min

Vegan Taco Soup

A hearty and flavorful Mexican-inspired soup.

Ingredients:

- 1 onion, chopped
- 1 bell pepper, chopped
- 2 cloves garlic, minced
- 1 cup corn kernels (fresh or frozen)
- 1 cup black beans, cooked
- 1 can diced tomatoes
- 4 cups vegetable broth
- 1 tbsp chili powder
- 1 tsp cumin
- Salt and pepper to taste

Directions

1. Sauté onion, bell pepper, and garlic until softened.
2. Add corn, black beans, diced tomatoes, vegetable broth, chili powder, and cumin.
3. Simmer for 20 minutes.
4. Season with salt and pepper.
5. Serve with your favorite taco toppings.
6. Enjoy your taco-inspired soup!

Substitutions

- Customize toppings with avocado, cilantro, or vegan cheese.
- Adjust spice level to taste.

4 servings   240   40 min

Italian Minestrone Soup

A classic Italian vegetable soup with pasta.

Ingredients:

- 1 onion, chopped
- 2 carrots, chopped
- 2 celery stalks, chopped
- 2 cloves garlic, minced
- 1 zucchini, diced
- 1 cup green beans, chopped
- 1 can diced tomatoes
- 1 cup cooked pasta
- 6 cups vegetable broth
- 1 tsp dried Italian herbs
- Salt and pepper to taste

Directions

1. Sauté onion, carrots, celery, and garlic until softened.
2. Add zucchini, green beans, diced tomatoes, pasta, vegetable broth, Italian herbs, salt, and pepper.
3. Simmer for 30 minutes.
4. Serve hot with a sprinkle of grated Parmesan cheese (or vegan alternative).
5. Enjoy your Italian minestrone!

Substitutions

- Use gluten-free pasta if needed.
- Add spinach or kale for extra greens.

4 servings   **300**   **45 min**

Vegan Gumbo

A rich and spicy Creole-inspired stew.

Ingredients:

- 1 onion, chopped
- 1 bell pepper, chopped
- 2 celery stalks, chopped
- 2 cloves garlic, minced
- 1 cup okra, sliced
- 1 cup canned chickpeas
- 1 cup canned kidney beans
- 1 cup canned diced tomatoes
- 4 cups vegetable broth
- 2 tsp Cajun seasoning
- Salt and pepper to taste

Directions

1. Sauté onion, bell pepper, celery, and garlic until softened.
2. Add okra, chickpeas, kidney beans, diced tomatoes, vegetable broth, Cajun seasoning, salt, and pepper.
3. Simmer for 30 minutes.
4. Serve over cooked rice or with crusty bread.
5. Enjoy the spicy flavors!

Substitutions

- Adjust spice level with Cajun seasoning.
- Add extra vegetables like bell peppers or corn.

4 servings | 250 | 35 min

Spinach and Lentil Soup

A nutritious soup with the goodness of lentils.

Ingredients:

- 1 cup dried green or brown lentils
- 1 onion, chopped
- 2 carrots, chopped
- 2 celery stalks, chopped
- 2 cloves garlic, minced
- 4 cups vegetable broth
- 2 cups fresh spinach
- 1 tsp dried thyme
- Salt and pepper to taste

Directions

1. Rinse lentils and cook until tender.
2. Sauté onion, carrots, celery, and garlic until softened.
3. Add cooked lentils, vegetable broth, spinach, thyme, salt, and pepper.
4. Simmer for 15 minutes until spinach wilts.
5. Enjoy the nutritious goodness!

Substitutions

- Use red lentils for a quicker cooking time.
- Add kale for extra greens.

4 servings | 350 | 40 min

Thai Peanut Noodle Soup

A creamy and savory Thai-inspired noodle soup.

Ingredients:

- 8 oz rice noodles
- 1 onion, chopped
- 2 cloves garlic, minced
- 1 bell pepper, sliced
- 1 cup sliced mushrooms
- 1 can coconut milk
- 4 cups vegetable broth
- 2 tbsp red curry paste
- 1 tbsp soy sauce
- 1 tbsp brown sugar
- Salt and pepper to taste

Directions

1. Cook rice noodles separately according to package instructions.
2. Sauté onion, garlic, bell pepper, and mushrooms until softened.
3. Add coconut milk, vegetable broth, red curry paste, soy sauce, brown sugar, salt, and pepper.
4. Simmer for 20 minutes.
5. Serve soup over cooked rice noodles.
6. Enjoy the creamy Thai flavors!

Substitutions

- Customize spice level with more or less red curry paste.
- Add tofu or tempeh for protein.

4 servings | 280 | 45 min

Vegan Borscht Soup

A vibrant and hearty Russian beet soup.

Ingredients:

- 2 large beets, peeled and grated
- 1 onion, chopped
- 2 carrots, chopped
- 2 cloves garlic, minced
- 4 cups vegetable broth
- 2 cups shredded cabbage
- 1 cup canned diced tomatoes
- 1 tbsp apple cider vinegar
- Salt and pepper to taste

Directions

1. Sauté onion, carrots, and garlic until softened.
2. Add grated beets, vegetable broth, cabbage, diced tomatoes, apple cider vinegar, salt, and pepper.
3. Simmer for 30 minutes until flavors meld.
4. Enjoy the vibrant borscht!

Substitutions

- Add a dollop of vegan sour cream for authenticity.
- Customize the acidity with more or less apple cider vinegar.

4 servings

320

30 min

Mexican Tortilla Soup

A spicy and comforting Mexican-inspired soup.

Ingredients:

- 1 onion, chopped
- 2 cloves garlic, minced
- 1 bell pepper, chopped
- 1 can black beans, drained and rinsed
- 1 can diced tomatoes
- 4 cups vegetable broth
- 1 tbsp chili powder
- 1 tsp cumin
- Salt and pepper to taste

Directions

1. Sauté onion, garlic, and bell pepper until softened.
2. Add black beans, diced tomatoes, vegetable broth, chili powder, cumin, salt, and pepper.
3. Simmer for 20 minutes.
4. Serve with tortilla chips and your choice of toppings.
5. Enjoy the Mexican flair!

Substitutions

- Customize toppings with avocado, cilantro, or vegan cheese.
- Adjust spice level to taste.

4 servings   290   35 min

Vegan Soba Noodle Soup

A Japanese-inspired noodle soup with a vegan twist.

Ingredients:

- 8 oz soba noodles
- 1 onion, sliced
- 2 cloves garlic, minced
- 4 cups vegetable broth
- 1 cup sliced mushrooms
- 1 cup sliced bok choy
- 1 cup sliced tofu
- 2 tbsp soy sauce
- 1 tsp sesame oil
- Green onions and nori for garnish

Directions

1. Cook soba noodles separately according to package instructions.
2. Sauté onion, garlic, and mushrooms until softened.
3. Add vegetable broth, bok choy, tofu, soy sauce, and sesame oil.
4. Simmer for 10 minutes.
5. Serve soup over cooked soba noodles.
6. Garnish with green onions and nori.
7. Enjoy your vegan soba noodle soup!

Substitutions

- Customize toppings with your favorite veggies and herbs.
- Adjust soy sauce for preferred saltiness.

4 servings | 270 | 40 min

Mediterranean Chickpea Soup

A Mediterranean-inspired soup with hearty chickpeas.

Ingredients:

- 2 cans chickpeas, drained and rinsed
- 1 onion, chopped
- 2 cloves garlic, minced
- 1 bell pepper, chopped
- 1 zucchini, chopped
- 1 can diced tomatoes
- 4 cups vegetable broth
- 2 tsp dried oregano
- Salt and pepper to taste

Directions

1. Sauté onion, garlic, bell pepper, and zucchini until softened.
2. Add chickpeas, diced tomatoes, vegetable broth, dried oregano, salt, and pepper.
3. Simmer for 20 minutes.
4. Enjoy the Mediterranean flavors!

Substitutions

- Add olives and feta cheese for extra Mediterranean flair.
- Customize vegetables with your favorites.

4 servings | 320 | 45 min

Vegan Eggplant Parmesan Soup

A comforting Italian-inspired soup with eggplant.

Ingredients:

- 1 large eggplant, diced
- 1 onion, chopped
- 2 cloves garlic, minced
- 1 can diced tomatoes
- 4 cups vegetable broth
- 1 cup cooked pasta
- 1/2 cup vegan mozzarella cheese, shredded
- 2 tbsp fresh basil leaves
- Salt and pepper to taste

Directions

1. Sauté eggplant, onion, and garlic until softened.
2. Add diced tomatoes, vegetable broth, cooked pasta, vegan mozzarella cheese, salt, and pepper.
3. Simmer for 30 minutes.
4. Serve hot with fresh basil leaves.
5. Enjoy your eggplant Parmesan soup!

Substitutions

- Use gluten-free pasta if needed.
- Customize cheese to your preference.

Chapter 6:
Satisfying Dinner Comforts

4 servings   250   30 min

Vegan Cream of Mushroom Soup

A creamy and savory mushroom delight.

Ingredients:

- 2 cups sliced mushrooms
- 1 onion, chopped
- 2 cloves garlic, minced
- 1/2 cup cashews, soaked
- 4 cups vegetable broth
- 1 cup unsweetened almond milk
- 2 tbsp nutritional yeast
- 1 tsp thyme
- Salt and pepper to taste

Directions

1. Sauté mushrooms, onion, and garlic until tender.
2. Blend cashews, vegetable broth, almond milk, nutritional yeast, thyme, salt, and pepper until smooth.
3. Pour the blended mixture into the sautéed mushrooms.
4. Simmer for 10 minutes, stirring occasionally.
5. Enjoy the creamy mushroom goodness!

Substitutions

- Use any plant-based milk you prefer.
- Adjust thyme to taste.

4 servings **320** **45 min**

Vegan Lasagna Soup

All the flavors of lasagna in a comforting soup.

Ingredients:

- 8 oz lasagna noodles
- 1 onion, chopped
- 2 cloves garlic, minced
- 1 bell pepper, chopped
- 1 cup sliced mushrooms
- 1 can crushed tomatoes
- 4 cups vegetable broth
- 1 tsp dried basil
- 1 tsp dried oregano
- Salt and pepper to taste

Directions

1. Cook lasagna noodles separately according to package instructions; set aside.
2. Sauté onion, garlic, bell pepper, and mushrooms until softened.
3. Add crushed tomatoes, vegetable broth, dried basil, dried oregano, salt, and pepper.
4. Simmer for 20 minutes.
5. Serve soup over cooked lasagna noodles.
6. Enjoy the lasagna-inspired goodness!

Substitutions

- Customize vegetables and herbs to your liking.
- Add vegan cheese for extra richness.

4 servings 350 50 min

Vegan Jambalaya

A spicy and flavorful Creole-inspired rice dish.

Ingredients:

- 1 cup brown rice
- 1 onion, chopped
- 2 cloves garlic, minced
- 1 bell pepper, chopped
- 1 cup sliced okra
- 1 cup canned kidney beans, drained
- 1 cup canned diced tomatoes
- 2 cups vegetable broth
- 1 tsp Cajun seasoning
- Salt and pepper to taste

Directions

1. Cook brown rice separately according to package instructions; set aside.
2. Sauté onion, garlic, bell pepper, and okra until softened.
3. Add kidney beans, diced tomatoes, vegetable broth, Cajun seasoning, salt, and pepper.
4. Simmer for 20 minutes.
5. Serve jambalaya over cooked brown rice.
6. Enjoy the spicy Creole flavors!

Substitutions

- Customize spice level with Cajun seasoning.
- Add vegan sausage for extra flavor.

4 servings   280   35 min

Vegan Creamy Potato Soup

A comforting and creamy potato-based soup.

Ingredients:

- 4 cups diced potatoes
- 1 onion, chopped
- 2 cloves garlic, minced
- 4 cups vegetable broth
- 1 cup unsweetened almond milk
- 2 tbsp nutritional yeast
- 1 tsp dried thyme
- Salt and pepper to taste

Directions

1. Boil diced potatoes until tender; set aside.
2. Sauté onion and garlic until softened.
3. Blend boiled potatoes, sautéed onion, vegetable broth, almond milk, nutritional yeast, thyme, salt, and pepper until creamy.
4. Reheat the soup, if needed.
5. Enjoy the creamy potato goodness!

Substitutions

- Use any plant-based milk you prefer.
- Adjust thyme to taste.

4 servings **320** **45 min**

A hearty and savory pie-inspired soup.

Vegan Shepherd's Pie Soup

Ingredients:

- 1 cup green lentils
- 1 onion, chopped
- 2 cloves garlic, minced
- 2 carrots, chopped
- 2 cups diced potatoes
- 4 cups vegetable broth
- 1 cup frozen peas
- 1 tsp dried thyme
- Mashed potatoes for topping
- Salt and pepper to taste

Directions

1. Cook green lentils separately until tender; set aside.
2. Sauté onion, garlic, carrots, and diced potatoes until softened.
3. Add vegetable broth, cooked lentils, frozen peas, dried thyme, salt, and pepper.
4. Simmer for 20 minutes.
5. Serve with a dollop of mashed potatoes on top.
6. Enjoy the hearty shepherd's pie-inspired soup!

Substitutions

- Customize vegetables and herbs to your liking.
- Use mashed cauliflower for a lighter topping.

4 servings | 220 | 30 min

Vegan Cabbage Soup

A simple and nutritious cabbage-based soup.

Ingredients:

- 4 cups shredded cabbage
- 1 onion, chopped
- 2 cloves garlic, minced
- 2 carrots, chopped
- 4 cups vegetable broth
- 1 cup diced tomatoes
- 1 tsp paprika
- 1 tsp dried thyme
- Salt and pepper to taste

Directions

1. Sauté onion and garlic until softened.
2. Add shredded cabbage, carrots, vegetable broth, diced tomatoes, paprika, dried thyme, salt, and pepper.
3. Simmer for 15 minutes.
4. Enjoy the simple and nutritious cabbage goodness!

Substitutions

- Add beans or lentils for extra protein.
- Customize spices to your liking.

4 servings | 180 | 20 min

Vegan Egg Drop Soup

A comforting Chinese-inspired egg drop soup.

Ingredients:

- 4 cups vegetable broth
- 1/2 cup frozen corn kernels
- 1/2 cup frozen peas
- 2 tbsp soy sauce
- 1 tsp sesame oil
- 2 green onions, sliced
- 2 tbsp cornstarch mixed with 2 tbsp water
- 2 eggs, beaten
- Salt and pepper to taste

Directions

1. Bring vegetable broth to a simmer.
2. Add frozen corn, peas, soy sauce, sesame oil, and sliced green onions.
3. Stir in the cornstarch-water mixture to thicken.
4. Slowly drizzle beaten eggs into the soup while stirring gently to create ribbons.
5. Season with salt and pepper.
6. Enjoy the comforting egg drop soup!

Substitutions

- Customize with tofu or mushrooms for extra texture.
- Adjust soy sauce and sesame oil to taste.

4 servings   **290**   **35 min**

Vegan Tortilla Pie Soup

A Mexican-inspired tortilla pie in soup form.

Ingredients:

- 1 onion, chopped
- 2 cloves garlic, minced
- 1 bell pepper, chopped
- 1 cup corn kernels (fresh or frozen)
- 1 can black beans, drained and rinsed
- 1 can diced tomatoes
- 4 cups vegetable broth
- 1 tsp chili powder
- 1 tsp cumin
- Salt and pepper to taste

Substitutions

- Customize toppings with avocado, cilantro, or vegan cheese.
- Adjust spice level to taste.

Directions

1. Sauté onion, garlic, bell pepper until softened.
2. Add corn, black beans, diced tomatoes, vegetable broth, chili powder, cumin, salt, and pepper.
3. Simmer for 15 minutes.
4. Serve with tortilla strips on top.
5. Enjoy the Mexican tortilla pie flavors!

4 servings   **270**   **40 min**

Vegan Tomato and Basil Risotto Soup

Creamy tomato and basil risotto in soup form.

Ingredients:

- 1 cup Arborio rice
- 1 onion, chopped
- 2 cloves garlic, minced
- 1 can diced tomatoes
- 4 cups vegetable broth
- 1 cup unsweetened almond milk
- 1/4 cup fresh basil leaves, chopped
- Salt and pepper to taste

Directions

1. Sauté onion and garlic until softened.
2. Add Arborio rice, diced tomatoes, vegetable broth, almond milk, salt, and pepper.
3. Simmer for 30 minutes, stirring occasionally.
4. Stir in chopped fresh basil.
5. Enjoy the creamy tomato and basil risotto soup!

Substitutions

- Use any plant-based milk you prefer.
- Customize with vegan Parmesan cheese for extra flavor.

4 servings | 280 | 35 min

Vegan Mushroom Stroganoff Soup

A rich and creamy mushroom stroganoff in soup form.

Ingredients:

- 2 cups sliced mushrooms
- 1 onion, chopped
- 2 cloves garlic, minced
- 1 cup cooked pasta
- 4 cups vegetable broth
- 1 cup unsweetened almond milk
- 2 tbsp nutritional yeast
- 2 tsp Dijon mustard
- Salt and pepper to taste

Directions

1. Sauté mushrooms, onion, and garlic until tender.
2. Add cooked pasta, vegetable broth, almond milk, nutritional yeast, Dijon mustard, salt, and pepper.
3. Simmer for 15 minutes.
4. Enjoy the rich and creamy mushroom stroganoff soup!

Substitutions

- Use any plant-based milk you prefer.
- Customize with vegan sour cream for extra creaminess.

Chapter 7:
Energizing Breakfast Bowls

2 servings   300   15 min

Acai Bowl

A refreshing and antioxidant-packed breakfast.

Ingredients:

- 2 packs frozen acai puree
- 1 banana
- 1/2 cup frozen mixed berries
- 1/2 cup unsweetened almond milk
- 1 tbsp honey
- Toppings: granola, sliced bananas, berries, shredded coconut, chia seeds

Directions

1. Blend acai puree, banana, mixed berries, almond milk, and honey until smooth.
2. Pour into bowls.
3. Top with granola, sliced bananas, berries, shredded coconut, and chia seeds.
4. Enjoy the refreshing acai bowl!

Substitutions

- Use any preferred sweetener.
- Customize toppings to your liking.

2 servings   250   10 min

Dragon Fruit Smoothie Bowl

A vibrant and tropical breakfast delight.

Ingredients:

- 1 dragon fruit, flesh scooped out
- 1 banana
- 1/2 cup frozen pineapple chunks
- 1/2 cup coconut milk
- Toppings: sliced dragon fruit, kiwi, granola, shredded coconut, chia seeds

Directions

1. Blend dragon fruit flesh, banana, frozen pineapple chunks, and coconut milk until smooth.
2. Pour into bowls.
3. Top with sliced dragon fruit, kiwi, granola, shredded coconut, and chia seeds.
4. Enjoy the vibrant dragon fruit smoothie bowl!

Substitutions

- Use any preferred milk or yogurt.
- Customize toppings with tropical fruits.

2 servings | 350 | 15 min

Chocolate Peanut Butter Breakfast Soup

A decadent and protein-packed breakfast treat.

Ingredients:

- 2 ripe bananas
- 2 tbsp peanut butter
- 2 tbsp cocoa powder
- 1/2 cup rolled oats
- 1 1/2 cups unsweetened almond milk
- 1 tbsp honey
- Toppings: sliced bananas, chopped peanuts, chocolate chips, drizzle of peanut butter

Directions

1. Blend ripe bananas, peanut butter, cocoa powder, rolled oats, almond milk, and honey until smooth.
2. Pour into bowls.
3. Top with sliced bananas, chopped peanuts, chocolate chips, and a drizzle of peanut butter.
4. Enjoy the indulgent chocolate peanut butter breakfast soup!

Substitutions

- Use any preferred nut butter.
- Customize toppings to your liking.

2 servings   **280**   **10 min**

Mango Turmeric Breakfast Soup

A tropical and anti-inflammatory breakfast.

Ingredients:

- 2 ripe mangoes, peeled and diced
- 1 banana
- 1/2 tsp ground turmeric
- 1/2 tsp ground ginger
- 1/2 cup Greek yogurt
- 1/2 cup coconut water
- 1 tbsp honey
- Toppings: diced mango, toasted coconut flakes, chia seeds

Directions

1. Blend ripe mangoes, banana, ground turmeric, ground ginger, Greek yogurt, coconut water, and honey until smooth.
2. Pour into bowls.
3. Top with diced mango, toasted coconut flakes, and chia seeds.
4. Enjoy the tropical mango turmeric breakfast soup!

Substitutions

- Use any preferred yogurt or dairy-free alternative.
- Customize toppings with tropical fruits.

2 servings | 230 | 10 min

A classic and refreshing berry breakfast.

Strawberry Banana Breakfast Soup

Ingredients:

- 1 cup fresh strawberries
- 2 ripe bananas
- 1/2 cup Greek yogurt
- 1/2 cup almond milk
- 1 tbsp honey
- Toppings: sliced strawberries, banana slices, granola, drizzle of honey, mint leaves

Directions

1. Blend fresh strawberries, ripe bananas, Greek yogurt, almond milk, and honey until smooth.
2. Pour into bowls.
3. Top with sliced strawberries, banana slices, granola, a drizzle of honey, and mint leaves.
4. Enjoy the classic strawberry banana breakfast soup!

Substitutions

- Use any preferred yogurt or dairy-free alternative.
- Customize toppings to your liking.

2 servings | 280 | 10 min

A creamy and green powerhouse breakfast.

Avocado and Spinach Breakfast Soup

Ingredients:

- 1 ripe avocado
- 1 cup fresh spinach leaves
- 1 banana
- 1/2 cup unsweetened almond milk
- 1 tbsp honey
- Toppings: sliced banana, fresh berries, hemp seeds, drizzle of honey

Directions

1. Blend ripe avocado, fresh spinach leaves, banana, almond milk, and honey until creamy.
2. Pour into bowls.
3. Top with sliced banana, fresh berries, hemp seeds, and a drizzle of honey.
4. Enjoy the creamy avocado and spinach breakfast soup!

Substitutions

- Use any preferred sweetener.
- Customize toppings with your favorite fruits and seeds.

2 servings   260   10 min

Kiwi and Pineapple Breakfast Soup

A tropical and vitamin C-packed breakfast.

Ingredients:

- 2 kiwis, peeled and diced
- 1 cup fresh pineapple chunks
- 1 banana
- 1/2 cup coconut water
- 1/2 cup Greek yogurt
- 1 tbsp honey
- Toppings: diced kiwi, pineapple chunks, shredded coconut, chia seeds

Directions

1. Blend diced kiwis, fresh pineapple chunks, banana, coconut water, Greek yogurt, and honey until smooth.
2. Pour into bowls.
3. Top with diced kiwi, pineapple chunks, shredded coconut, and chia seeds.
4. Enjoy the tropical kiwi and pineapple breakfast soup!

Substitutions

- Use any preferred yogurt or dairy-free alternative.
- Customize toppings with tropical fruits.

2 servings | 320 | 10 min

Cherry Almond Breakfast Soup

A fruity and nutty morning delight.

Ingredients:

- 1 cup fresh or frozen cherries
- 1/2 cup almond butter
- 1 banana
- 1/2 cup almond milk
- 1 tbsp honey
- Toppings: fresh cherries, sliced almonds, drizzle of honey

Directions

1. Blend fresh or frozen cherries, almond butter, banana, almond milk, and honey until smooth.
2. Pour into bowls.
3. Top with fresh cherries, sliced almonds, and a drizzle of honey.
4. Enjoy the fruity and nutty cherry almond breakfast soup!

Substitutions

- Use any preferred nut butter.
- Customize toppings with your favorite fruits and nuts.

2 servings   290   10 min

Peach Cobbler Breakfast Soup

A sweet and peachy breakfast reminiscent of cobbler.

Ingredients:

- 2 ripe peaches, peeled and diced
- 1 banana
- 1/2 cup rolled oats
- 1/2 cup almond milk
- 1 tbsp honey
- 1/2 tsp ground cinnamon
- Toppings: diced peaches, granola, chopped walnuts, drizzle of honey

Directions

1. Blend ripe peaches, banana, rolled oats, almond milk, honey, and ground cinnamon until smooth.
2. Pour into bowls.
3. Top with diced peaches, granola, chopped walnuts, and a drizzle of honey.
4. Enjoy the sweet peach cobbler breakfast soup!

Substitutions

- Customize toppings with your favorite nuts and sweeteners.
- Add a pinch of nutmeg for extra flavor.

2 servings   250   15 min

Raspberry Chia Breakfast Soup

A nutritious and berry-packed breakfast.

Ingredients:

- 1 cup fresh raspberries
- 2 tbsp chia seeds
- 1 banana
- 1/2 cup almond milk
- 1 tbsp honey
- Toppings: fresh raspberries, chia seeds, sliced banana, drizzle of honey

Directions

1. Blend fresh raspberries, chia seeds, banana, almond milk, and honey until smooth.
2. Pour into bowls.
3. Top with fresh raspberries, chia seeds, sliced banana, and a drizzle of honey.
4. Enjoy the nutritious raspberry chia breakfast soup!

Substitutions

- Customize toppings with your favorite berries and seeds.
- Use any preferred sweetener.

Chapter 8:
Flavorful Lunchtime Classics

 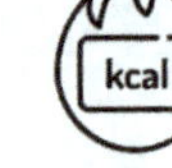 

4 servings 320 40 min

Vegan Clam Chowder

A creamy and seafood-inspired chowder.

Ingredients:

- 1 can young jackfruit, drained and shredded
- 1 onion, chopped
- 2 cloves garlic, minced
- 2 celery stalks, chopped
- 2 carrots, chopped
- 4 cups vegetable broth
- 1 cup unsweetened almond milk
- 1/4 cup cashews, soaked
- 2 tbsp nutritional yeast
- 2 tbsp vegan butter
- 1 tsp dried thyme
- Salt and pepper to taste

Substitutions

- Use hearts of palm or artichoke hearts as a clam substitute.
- Adjust thyme to taste.

Directions

1. Sauté shredded jackfruit, onion, garlic, celery, and carrots until softened.
2. Add vegetable broth and simmer until vegetables are tender.
3. Blend soaked cashews, almond milk, nutritional yeast, and vegan butter until creamy.
4. Stir the cashew mixture into the soup.
5. Season with dried thyme, salt, and pepper.
6. Enjoy the vegan clam chowder!

4 servings   **350**   **50 min**

Vegan Goulash Soup

A hearty and spiced Hungarian-inspired soup.

Ingredients:

- 2 cups seitan or tempeh, diced
- 1 onion, chopped
- 2 cloves garlic, minced
- 1 bell pepper, chopped
- 1 can diced tomatoes
- 4 cups vegetable broth
- 2 tsp smoked paprika
- 1 tsp caraway seeds
- Salt and pepper to taste

Directions

1. Sauté diced seitan or tempeh, onion, garlic, and bell pepper until browned.
2. Add diced tomatoes, vegetable broth, smoked paprika, and caraway seeds.
3. Simmer for 30 minutes.
4. Enjoy the hearty vegan goulash soup!

Substitutions

- Use tofu or mushrooms for protein if preferred.
- Customize spices to your liking.

4 servings   280   35 min

A comforting and tomato-based rice soup.

Vegan Tomato Rice Soup

Ingredients:

- 1 cup white rice
- 1 onion, chopped
- 2 cloves garlic, minced
- 1 can diced tomatoes
- 4 cups vegetable broth
- 1 tsp dried basil
- 1 tsp dried oregano
- Salt and pepper to taste

Directions

1. Cook white rice separately according to package instructions; set aside.
2. Sauté onion and garlic until softened.
3. Add diced tomatoes, vegetable broth, dried basil, dried oregano, salt, and pepper.
4. Simmer for 20 minutes.
5. Serve soup over cooked white rice.
6. Enjoy the comforting vegan tomato rice soup!

Substitutions

- Customize herbs to your liking.
- Add tofu or chickpeas for extra protein.

4 servings | 320 | 45 min

Vegan Thai Green Curry Soup

A flavorful and spicy Thai-inspired soup.

Ingredients:

- 1 cup brown rice
- 1 can coconut milk
- 2 tbsp Thai green curry paste
- 1 bell pepper, sliced
- 1 zucchini, sliced
- 1 cup sliced mushrooms
- 4 cups vegetable broth
- 1 tbsp soy sauce
- 1 tsp brown sugar
- Juice of 1 lime
- Fresh cilantro for garnish

Substitutions

- Customize spice level with curry paste.
- Add tofu or tempeh for extra protein.

Directions

1. Cook brown rice separately according to package instructions; set aside.
2. In a pot, simmer coconut milk and Thai green curry paste for 5 minutes.
3. Add sliced bell pepper, zucchini, mushrooms, vegetable broth, soy sauce, and brown sugar.
4. Simmer for 20 minutes.
5. Stir in lime juice.
6. Serve soup over cooked brown rice.
7. Garnish with fresh cilantro.
8. Enjoy the flavorful vegan Thai green curry soup!

 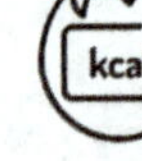 

4 servings   280   40 min

Vegan Sweet Potato Bisque

A creamy and sweet potato-based bisque.

Ingredients:

- 2 large sweet potatoes, peeled and diced
- 1 onion, chopped
- 2 cloves garlic, minced
- 4 cups vegetable broth
- 1 cup unsweetened almond milk
- 2 tbsp nutritional yeast
- 1 tsp dried thyme
- Salt and pepper to taste

Directions

1. Boil diced sweet potatoes until tender; set aside.
2. Sauté onion and garlic until softened.
3. Blend boiled sweet potatoes, sautéed onion, vegetable broth, almond milk, nutritional yeast, and dried thyme until creamy.
4. Reheat the bisque if needed.
5. Season with salt and pepper.
6. Enjoy the creamy vegan sweet potato bisque!

Substitutions

- Use any preferred plant-based milk.
- Customize herbs to your liking.

4 servings | 250 | 30 min

Vegan Roasted Garlic Soup

A rich and garlicky soup with a roasted twist.

Ingredients:

- 2 whole garlic bulbs
- 1 onion, chopped
- 2 cloves garlic, minced
- 4 cups vegetable broth
- 1/2 cup unsweetened almond milk
- 2 tbsp olive oil
- 1 tsp dried thyme
- Salt and pepper to taste

Directions

1. Preheat the oven to 400°F (200°C).
2. Cut the tops off the garlic bulbs, drizzle with olive oil, and roast for 30 minutes until soft.
3. Squeeze out roasted garlic cloves.
4. In a pot, sauté chopped onion and minced garlic until softened.
5. Add roasted garlic, vegetable broth, almond milk, dried thyme, salt, and pepper.
6. Simmer for 10 minutes.
7. Enjoy the rich vegan roasted garlic soup!

Substitutions

- Customize herbs and spices to your liking.
- Drizzle with truffle oil for extra flavor.

4 servings   280   35 min

Vegan Pumpkin and Sage Soup

A comforting autumn-inspired pumpkin soup.

Ingredients:

- 2 cups canned pumpkin puree
- 1 onion, chopped
- 2 cloves garlic, minced
- 4 cups vegetable broth
- 1/2 cup unsweetened almond milk
- 2 tbsp nutritional yeast
- 1 tsp dried sage
- Salt and pepper to taste

Directions

1. Sauté chopped onion and minced garlic until softened.
2. Add pumpkin puree, vegetable broth, almond milk, nutritional yeast, dried sage, salt, and pepper.
3. Simmer for 15 minutes.
4. Enjoy the comforting vegan pumpkin and sage soup!

Substitutions

- Use any preferred plant-based milk.
- Customize herbs to your liking.

4 servings

320

30 min

Vegan Spinach and Artichoke Soup

A creamy and spinach-artichoke dip-inspired soup.

Ingredients:

- 1 can artichoke hearts, drained and chopped
- 4 cups fresh spinach leaves
- 1 onion, chopped
- 2 cloves garlic, minced
- 1 cup unsweetened almond milk
- 2 cups vegetable broth
- 2 tbsp nutritional yeast
- 1/2 cup vegan cream cheese
- Salt and pepper to taste

Directions

1. Sauté chopped artichoke hearts, fresh spinach, onion, and minced garlic until spinach wilts.
2. Add almond milk, vegetable broth, nutritional yeast, vegan cream cheese, salt, and pepper.
3. Simmer for 10 minutes, stirring occasionally.
4. Enjoy the creamy vegan spinach and artichoke soup!

Substitutions

- Use any preferred plant-based milk and cream cheese.
- Customize with extra herbs and spices.

4 servings   290   35 min

Vegan Corn and Potato Chowder

A hearty and corn-filled potato chowder.

Ingredients:

- 2 cups diced potatoes
- 1 onion, chopped
- 2 cloves garlic, minced
- 2 cups corn kernels (fresh or frozen)
- 4 cups vegetable broth
- 1 cup unsweetened almond milk
- 1/4 cup vegan cheddar cheese shreds
- 1 tsp dried thyme
- Salt and pepper to taste

Directions

1. Boil diced potatoes until tender; set aside.
2. Sauté chopped onion and minced garlic until softened.
3. Add corn kernels, vegetable broth, almond milk, vegan cheddar cheese shreds, dried thyme, salt, and pepper.
4. Simmer for 15 minutes.
5. Stir in boiled potatoes.
6. Enjoy the hearty vegan corn and potato chowder!

Substitutions

- Use any preferred plant-based milk and cheese shreds.
- Customize with diced bell peppers for extra color.

4 servings   300   40 min

Vegan Lentil and Kale Soup

A nutritious and hearty lentil and kale soup.

Ingredients:

- 1 cup dried green or brown lentils
- 1 onion, chopped
- 2 cloves garlic, minced
- 2 carrots, chopped
- 2 cups chopped kale leaves
- 4 cups vegetable broth
- 1 tsp cumin
- 1 tsp smoked paprika
- Salt and pepper to taste

Directions

1. Rinse dried lentils and set aside.
2. Sauté chopped onion and minced garlic until softened.
3. Add dried lentils, chopped carrots, chopped kale, vegetable broth, cumin, smoked paprika, salt, and pepper.
4. Simmer for 30 minutes, or until lentils are tender.
5. Enjoy the nutritious vegan lentil and kale soup!

Substitutions

- Customize spices to your liking.
- Add diced tomatoes for extra flavor.

Chapter 9:
Cozy Dinner Soups

4 servings   280   40 min

Vegan Creamy Asparagus Soup

A velvety and indulgent asparagus delight.

Ingredients:

- 1 lb fresh asparagus, trimmed and chopped
- 1 onion, chopped
- 2 cloves garlic, minced
- 4 cups vegetable broth
- 1 cup unsweetened almond milk
- 2 tbsp vegan butter
- 2 tbsp all-purpose flour
- 1 tsp dried thyme
- Salt and pepper to taste

Directions

1. Sauté chopped asparagus, onion, and minced garlic until tender.
2. Melt vegan butter in the pot and stir in all-purpose flour to make a roux.
3. Gradually whisk in vegetable broth until smooth.
4. Add sautéed vegetables, almond milk, dried thyme, salt, and pepper.
5. Simmer for 20 minutes.
6. Enjoy the velvety vegan creamy asparagus soup!

Substitutions

- Use any preferred plant-based milk.
- Customize herbs to your liking.

4 servings 350 50 min

Vegan Stuffed Bell Pepper Soup

All the flavors of stuffed bell peppers in a soup.

Ingredients:

- 2 bell peppers, chopped
- 1 onion, chopped
- 2 cloves garlic, minced
- 1 cup cooked rice
- 1 can diced tomatoes
- 4 cups vegetable broth
- 1 tsp dried oregano
- Salt and pepper to taste

Directions

1. Sauté chopped bell peppers, onion, and minced garlic until softened.
2. Add cooked rice, diced tomatoes, vegetable broth, dried oregano, salt, and pepper.
3. Simmer for 20 minutes.
4. Enjoy the flavors of stuffed bell peppers in this vegan soup!

Substitutions

- Customize with your favorite grains.
- Add beans or lentils for extra protein.

4 servings **320** **45 min**

Vegan Cajun Red Beans and Rice Soup

A spicy and hearty Cajun-inspired soup.

Ingredients:

- 1 cup cooked red beans
- 1 cup cooked rice
- 1 onion, chopped
- 2 cloves garlic, minced
- 1 bell pepper, chopped
- 4 cups vegetable broth
- 2 tsp Cajun seasoning
- 1/2 tsp cayenne pepper (adjust to spice preference)
- Salt and pepper to taste

Directions

1. Sauté chopped onion, minced garlic, and bell pepper until softened.
2. Add cooked red beans, cooked rice, vegetable broth, Cajun seasoning, cayenne pepper, salt, and pepper.
3. Simmer for 20 minutes.
4. Enjoy the spicy and hearty vegan Cajun red beans and rice soup!

Substitutions

- Customize spice level to taste.
- Add vegan sausage for extra flavor.

 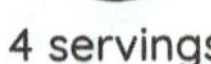  

4 servings   **290**   **40 min**

Vegan Ratatouille Soup

A rustic and vegetable-packed French classic.

Ingredients:

- 1 eggplant, diced
- 2 zucchinis, diced
- 1 bell pepper, diced
- 1 onion, chopped
- 2 cloves garlic, minced
- 1 can diced tomatoes
- 4 cups vegetable broth
- 1 tsp dried thyme
- 1 tsp dried basil
- Salt and pepper to taste

Directions

1. Sauté diced eggplant, zucchinis, bell pepper, chopped onion, and minced garlic until tender.
2. Add diced tomatoes, vegetable broth, dried thyme, dried basil, salt, and pepper.
3. Simmer for 20 minutes.
4. Enjoy the rustic vegan ratatouille soup!

Substitutions

- Customize herbs to your liking.
- Add chickpeas for extra protein.

4 servings | 280 | 30 min

Vegan Creamy Pesto Zucchini Soup

A creamy and basil-infused zucchini soup.

Ingredients:

- 4 cups sliced zucchini
- 1 onion, chopped
- 2 cloves garlic, minced
- 4 cups vegetable broth
- 1/2 cup unsweetened almond milk
- 2 tbsp vegan pesto
- 1 tbsp nutritional yeast
- Salt and pepper to taste

Directions

1. Sauté sliced zucchini, chopped onion, and minced garlic until tender.
2. Add vegetable broth, almond milk, vegan pesto, nutritional yeast, salt, and pepper.
3. Simmer for 15 minutes.
4. Enjoy the creamy vegan pesto zucchini soup!

Substitutions

- Use any preferred plant-based milk.
- Customize with extra basil for a stronger pesto flavor.

4 servings   320   45 min

Vegan Korean Kimchi Soup

A spicy and umami-rich Korean-inspired kimchi soup.

Ingredients:

- 1 cup kimchi, chopped
- 1 onion, chopped
- 2 cloves garlic, minced
- 4 cups vegetable broth
- 1 cup kimchi juice (from the jar)
- 2 tbsp gochujang (Korean red pepper paste)
- 1 tsp sesame oil
- 1 tsp soy sauce
- 1/2 cup sliced tofu
- 2 green onions, sliced
- Salt and pepper to taste

Substitutions

- Adjust gochujang to spice preference.
- Customize with mushrooms or noodles for variation.

Directions

1. Sauté chopped kimchi, chopped onion, and minced garlic until fragrant.
2. Add vegetable broth, kimchi juice, gochujang, sesame oil, soy sauce, salt, and pepper.
3. Simmer for 20 minutes.
4. Stir in sliced tofu and green onions.
5. Enjoy the spicy and umami-rich vegan Korean kimchi soup!

4 servings   290   45 min

Vegan Cuban Black Bean Soup

A hearty and flavorful Cuban-inspired black bean soup.

Ingredients:

- 2 cans black beans, drained and rinsed
- 1 onion, chopped
- 2 cloves garlic, minced
- 1 bell pepper, chopped
- 1 carrot, chopped
- 4 cups vegetable broth
- 2 tsp ground cumin
- 1 tsp smoked paprika
- Salt and pepper to taste

Directions

1. Sauté chopped onion, minced garlic, bell pepper, and carrot until softened.
2. Add black beans, vegetable broth, ground cumin, smoked paprika, salt, and pepper.
3. Simmer for 20 minutes.
4. Enjoy the hearty vegan Cuban black bean soup!

Substitutions

- Customize with extra spices for a bolder flavor.
- Serve with a dollop of vegan sour cream.

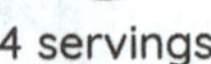

4 servings

320

40 min

Vegan Thai Basil Eggplant Soup

A fragrant and Thai-inspired eggplant soup.

Ingredients:

- 2 cups diced eggplant
- 1 onion, chopped
- 2 cloves garlic, minced
- 1 can coconut milk
- 4 cups vegetable broth
- 2 tbsp Thai basil leaves (fresh or dried)
- 1 tsp red curry paste (adjust to spice preference)
- Salt and pepper to taste

Directions

1. Sauté diced eggplant, chopped onion, and minced garlic until tender.
2. Add coconut milk, vegetable broth, Thai basil leaves, red curry paste, salt, and pepper.
3. Simmer for 20 minutes.
4. Enjoy the fragrant vegan Thai basil eggplant soup!

Substitutions

- Customize spice level with red curry paste.
- Use fresh Thai basil for a stronger flavor.

4 servings   **350**   **35 min**

Vegan Mushroom and Spinach Tortellini Soup

A comforting and tortellini-filled mushroom soup.

Ingredients:

- 2 cups vegan cheese or spinach tortellini
- 8 oz mushrooms, sliced
- 1 onion, chopped
- 2 cloves garlic, minced
- 4 cups vegetable broth
- 2 cups unsweetened almond milk
- 2 tbsp vegan cream cheese
- 1 tsp dried thyme
- Salt and pepper to taste

Directions

1. Cook tortellini separately according to package instructions; set aside.
2. Sauté sliced mushrooms, chopped onion, and minced garlic until tender.
3. Add vegetable broth, almond milk, vegan cream cheese, dried thyme, salt, and pepper.
4. Simmer for 15 minutes.
5. Stir in cooked tortellini.
6. Enjoy the comforting vegan mushroom and spinach tortellini soup!

Substitutions

- Use any preferred plant-based milk and tortellini flavor.
- Customize with fresh herbs.

4 servings · 320 · 40 min

A creamy and pasta-infused Alfredo soup.

Vegan Alfredo Pasta Soup

Ingredients:

- 2 cups cooked pasta (penne or fettuccine)
- 1 onion, chopped
- 2 cloves garlic, minced
- 4 cups vegetable broth
- 1 cup unsweetened almond milk
- 1/4 cup vegan Alfredo sauce
- 2 tbsp nutritional yeast
- Salt and pepper to taste

Directions

1. Cook pasta separately according to package instructions; set aside.
2. Sauté chopped onion and minced garlic until softened.
3. Add vegetable broth, almond milk, vegan Alfredo sauce, nutritional yeast, salt, and pepper.
4. Simmer for 15 minutes.
5. Stir in cooked pasta.
6. Enjoy the creamy vegan Alfredo pasta soup!

Substitutions

- Use any preferred plant-based milk and pasta shape.
- Customize with extra herbs and spices.

Chapter 10:
Nourishing Breakfast Starters

4 servings **350** **45 min**

Vegan Breakfast Burrito Soup

All the flavors of a breakfast burrito in a soup.

Ingredients:

- 1 cup cooked brown rice
- 1 cup cooked black beans
- 1 bell pepper, chopped
- 1 onion, chopped
- 2 cloves garlic, minced
- 1 can diced tomatoes with green chilies
- 4 cups vegetable broth
- 1 tsp ground cumin
- 1 tsp chili powder
- Salt and pepper to taste

Directions

1. Sauté chopped bell pepper, chopped onion, and minced garlic until softened.
2. Add cooked brown rice, cooked black beans, diced tomatoes with green chilies, vegetable broth, ground cumin, chili powder, salt, and pepper.
3. Simmer for 20 minutes.
4. Enjoy the flavors of a breakfast burrito in this vegan soup!

Substitutions

- Customize with your favorite breakfast burrito fillings.
- Add avocado and vegan sour cream as toppings.

4 servings   290   35 min

Vegan Blueberry Pancake Soup

A delightful blueberry pancake-inspired breakfast.

Ingredients:

- 1 cup rolled oats
- 1 cup almond milk
- 1/2 cup blueberries (fresh or frozen)
- 1 banana, mashed
- 2 tbsp maple syrup
- 1/2 tsp vanilla extract
- 1/2 tsp ground cinnamon
- 1/4 tsp nutmeg
- Toppings: additional blueberries, maple syrup, chopped nuts, and vegan whipped cream (optional)

Directions

1. Blend rolled oats, almond milk, blueberries, mashed banana, maple syrup, vanilla extract, ground cinnamon, and nutmeg until smooth.
2. Pour into bowls.
3. Top with additional blueberries, maple syrup, chopped nuts, and vegan whipped cream if desired.
4. Enjoy the delightful vegan blueberry pancake soup!

Substitutions

- Customize toppings with your favorite fruits and nuts.
- Use any preferred sweetener.

4 servings | 320 | 45 min

Vegan Breakfast Enchilada Soup

A Tex-Mex-inspired breakfast enchilada in soup form.

Ingredients:

- 1 cup cooked black beans
- 1 cup cooked brown rice
- 1 onion, chopped
- 2 cloves garlic, minced
- 1 can enchilada sauce
- 4 cups vegetable broth
- 1 tsp ground cumin
- 1 tsp chili powder
- Salt and pepper to taste

Directions

1. Sauté chopped onion and minced garlic until softened.
2. Add cooked black beans, cooked brown rice, enchilada sauce, vegetable broth, ground cumin, chili powder, salt, and pepper.
3. Simmer for 20 minutes.
4. Enjoy the Tex-Mex flavors of this vegan breakfast enchilada soup!

Substitutions

- Customize with your favorite enchilada fillings.
- Top with vegan cheese and avocado.

4 servings   350   50 min

Vegan Breakfast Quesadilla Soup

A savory and cheesy breakfast quesadilla-inspired soup.

Ingredients:

- 1 cup cooked tofu scramble (tofu, veggies, and spices)
- 2 whole wheat tortillas, chopped
- 1 can diced tomatoes with green chilies
- 4 cups vegetable broth
- 1 cup vegan cheese shreds
- 1 tsp ground cumin
- 1 tsp chili powder
- Salt and pepper to taste

Directions

1. In a pot, combine cooked tofu scramble, chopped whole wheat tortillas, diced tomatoes with green chilies, vegetable broth, vegan cheese shreds, ground cumin, chili powder, salt, and pepper.
2. Simmer for 20 minutes.
3. Enjoy the savory and cheesy vegan breakfast quesadilla soup!

Substitutions

- Customize tofu scramble with your favorite veggies and spices.
- Use any preferred tortillas and vegan cheese.

4 servings   320   40 min

Vegan Tofu Scramble Soup

A protein-packed tofu scramble-inspired breakfast.

Ingredients:

- 1 cup cooked tofu scramble (tofu, veggies, and spices)
- 1 onion, chopped
- 2 cloves garlic, minced
- 4 cups vegetable broth
- 1 cup diced potatoes
- 1/2 cup diced bell peppers
- 1/2 cup diced tomatoes
- 1/2 cup chopped spinach
- 1/2 tsp turmeric
- Salt and pepper to taste

Directions

1. Sauté chopped onion and minced garlic until softened.
2. Add cooked tofu scramble, diced potatoes, diced bell peppers, diced tomatoes, chopped spinach, turmeric, vegetable broth, salt, and pepper.
3. Simmer for 20 minutes.
4. Enjoy the protein-packed vegan tofu scramble soup!

Substitutions

- Customize tofu scramble with your favorite veggies and spices.
- Add vegan cheese for extra flavor.

4 servings | 350 | 45 min

Vegan Breakfast Tacos Soup

All the goodness of breakfast tacos in a bowl.

Ingredients:

- 1 cup cooked black beans
- 1 cup cooked tofu scramble (tofu, veggies, and spices)
- 1 onion, chopped
- 2 cloves garlic, minced
- 1 can diced tomatoes with green chilies
- 4 cups vegetable broth
- 1 tsp ground cumin
- 1 tsp chili powder
- Salt and pepper to taste

Directions

1. Sauté chopped onion and minced garlic until softened.
2. Add cooked black beans, cooked tofu scramble, diced tomatoes with green chilies, vegetable broth, ground cumin, chili powder, salt, and pepper.
3. Simmer for 20 minutes.
4. Enjoy the flavors of breakfast tacos in this vegan soup!

Substitutions

- Customize tofu scramble with your favorite veggies and spices.
- Top with vegan sour cream and avocado.

4 servings | 320 | 35 min

Vegan Breakfast Sandwich Soup

A breakfast sandwich-inspired soup with a twist.

Ingredients:

- 2 whole wheat English muffins, chopped
- 1 onion, chopped
- 2 cloves garlic, minced
- 4 cups vegetable broth
- 1 cup chopped spinach
- 1 cup vegan sausage crumbles
- 1 cup vegan cheese shreds
- 1/2 tsp dried basil
- 1/2 tsp dried oregano
- Salt and pepper to taste

Directions

1. In a pot, combine chopped English muffins, chopped onion, minced garlic, vegetable broth, chopped spinach, vegan sausage crumbles, vegan cheese shreds, dried basil, dried oregano, salt, and pepper.
2. Simmer for 15 minutes.
3. Enjoy the unique twist of this vegan breakfast sandwich soup!

Substitutions

- Customize with your favorite vegan sausage and cheese.
- Add hot sauce for extra kick.

4 servings   330   40 min

Vegan Breakfast Hash Soup

A hearty breakfast hash-inspired soup.

Ingredients:

- 1 cup diced potatoes
- 1 onion, chopped
- 2 cloves garlic, minced
- 4 cups vegetable broth
- 1 cup cooked black beans
- 1 cup chopped bell peppers
- 1/2 cup chopped kale
- 1/2 tsp smoked paprika
- Salt and pepper to taste

Directions

1. Sauté diced potatoes, chopped onion, and minced garlic until potatoes are tender.
2. Add cooked black beans, chopped bell peppers, chopped kale, vegetable broth, smoked paprika, salt, and pepper.
3. Simmer for 20 minutes.
4. Enjoy the hearty vegan breakfast hash soup!

Substitutions

- Customize with your favorite veggies and spices.
- Add vegan cheese as a topping.

4 servings   340   45 min

Vegan Breakfast Pizza Soup

A pizza-inspired breakfast in soup form.

Ingredients:

- 2 whole wheat pizza crusts, chopped
- 1 onion, chopped
- 2 cloves garlic, minced
- 1 can tomato sauce
- 4 cups vegetable broth
- 1 cup vegan cheese shreds
- 1 tsp dried basil
- 1 tsp dried oregano
- Salt and pepper to taste

Directions

1. In a pot, combine chopped pizza crusts, chopped onion, minced garlic, tomato sauce, vegetable broth, vegan cheese shreds, dried basil, dried oregano, salt, and pepper.
2. Simmer for 15 minutes.
3. Enjoy the pizza-inspired vegan breakfast pizza soup!

Substitutions

- Customize with your favorite pizza toppings.
- Add vegan pepperoni or mushrooms for variation.

 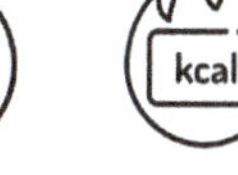 

4 servings

330

40 min

Vegan Breakfast Wrap Soup

A breakfast wrap-inspired soup with a twist.

Ingredients:

- 2 whole wheat tortillas, chopped
- 1 cup cooked tofu scramble (tofu, veggies, and spices)
- 1 can black beans, drained and rinsed
- 4 cups vegetable broth
- 1 cup vegan cheese shreds
- 1 tsp ground cumin
- 1/2 tsp chili powder
- Salt and pepper to taste

Directions

1. In a pot, combine chopped tortillas, cooked tofu scramble, black beans, vegetable broth, vegan cheese shreds, ground cumin, chili powder, salt, and pepper.
2. Simmer for 15 minutes.
3. Enjoy the twist of this vegan breakfast wrap soup!

Substitutions

- Customize tofu scramble with your favorite veggies and spices.
- Top with vegan sour cream and salsa.

Chapter 11:
Revitalizing Breakfast Soups

4 servings | 320 | 45 min

Vegan Blueberry Muffin Soup

A delightful blueberry muffin-inspired breakfast.

~~~~~~~~~~~~~~~

Ingredients:

- 1 cup rolled oats
- 1 cup almond milk
- 1/2 cup blueberries (fresh or frozen)
- 1 banana, mashed
- 2 tbsp maple syrup
- 1/2 tsp vanilla extract
- 1/2 tsp ground cinnamon
- 1/4 tsp nutmeg
- Toppings: additional blueberries, maple syrup, chopped nuts, and vegan whipped cream (optional)

Directions

1. Blend rolled oats, almond milk, blueberries, mashed banana, maple syrup, vanilla extract, ground cinnamon, and nutmeg until smooth.
2. Pour into bowls.
3. Top with additional blueberries, maple syrup, chopped nuts, and vegan whipped cream if desired.
4. Enjoy the delightful vegan blueberry muffin soup!

Substitutions

- Customize toppings with your favorite fruits and nuts.
- Use any preferred sweetener.
~~~~~~~~~~~~~~~

4 servings   **340**   **40 min**

Vegan Breakfast BLT Soup

A savory and satisfying breakfast BLT-inspired soup.

Ingredients:

- 1 cup vegan bacon bits
- 1 cup cherry tomatoes, halved
- 4 cups vegetable broth
- 1 cup chopped lettuce
- 1/2 cup vegan mayo
- 1/4 cup vegan cream cheese
- 1 tsp dried basil
- Salt and pepper to taste

Directions

1. In a pot, combine vegan bacon bits, cherry tomatoes, vegetable broth, chopped lettuce, vegan mayo, vegan cream cheese, dried basil, salt, and pepper.
2. Simmer for 15 minutes.
3. Enjoy the savory and satisfying vegan breakfast BLT soup!

Substitutions

- Customize with your favorite vegan bacon alternative.
- Add avocado for extra flavor.

4 servings

320

35 min

Vegan Breakfast Bowl Soup

A customizable breakfast bowl-inspired soup.

Ingredients:

- 2 cups cooked quinoa
- 1 cup mixed berries (strawberries, blueberries, raspberries)
- 1 banana, sliced
- 1/4 cup chopped nuts (almonds, walnuts, or pecans)
- 1/4 cup unsweetened almond milk
- 2 tbsp maple syrup
- 1/2 tsp vanilla extract
- Toppings: vegan yogurt and a drizzle of honey (optional)

Directions

1. In a pot, combine cooked quinoa, mixed berries, sliced banana, chopped nuts, unsweetened almond milk, maple syrup, and vanilla extract.
2. Heat gently, stirring until heated through.
3. Pour into bowls.
4. Top with vegan yogurt and a drizzle of honey if desired.
5. Enjoy the customizable vegan breakfast bowl soup!

Substitutions

- Customize with your favorite fruits, nuts, and toppings.
- Use any preferred sweetener.

4 servings   350   45 min

Vegan Breakfast Sushi Soup

A creative and sushi-inspired breakfast soup.

Ingredients:

- 2 cups cooked sushi rice
- 1/2 cup avocado, sliced
- 1/2 cup cucumber, sliced
- 1/2 cup carrots, julienned
- 1/2 cup bell peppers, thinly sliced
- 4 sheets nori (seaweed) paper, torn into pieces
- 1/4 cup pickled ginger
- 1/4 cup soy sauce
- 1 tbsp rice vinegar
- Sesame seeds and wasabi for garnish (optional)

Substitutions

- Customize with your favorite sushi ingredients.
- Adjust soy sauce to taste.

Directions

1. In a pot, combine cooked sushi rice, avocado, cucumber, carrots, bell peppers, nori paper pieces, pickled ginger, soy sauce, and rice vinegar.
2. Heat gently, stirring until heated through.
3. Serve in bowls.
4. Garnish with sesame seeds and wasabi if desired.
5. Enjoy the creative vegan breakfast sushi soup!

4 servings

310

35 min

Vegan Breakfast Bruschetta Soup

A refreshing bruschetta-inspired breakfast soup.

Ingredients:

- 4 cups diced tomatoes
- 1/2 cup chopped fresh basil
- 1/4 cup chopped red onion
- 2 cloves garlic, minced
- 1/4 cup balsamic vinegar
- 1/4 cup olive oil
- Salt and pepper to taste
- Toasted bread cubes for garnish (optional)

Directions

1. In a pot, combine diced tomatoes, chopped fresh basil, chopped red onion, minced garlic, balsamic vinegar, and olive oil.
2. Heat gently, stirring until heated through.
3. Season with salt and pepper to taste.
4. Serve in bowls.
5. Garnish with toasted bread cubes if desired.
6. Enjoy the refreshing vegan breakfast bruschetta soup!

Substitutions

- Customize with your favorite herbs and spices.
- Drizzle with balsamic reduction for extra flavor.

4 servings | 360 | 40 min

Vegan Breakfast Nachos Soup

A nacho-inspired breakfast soup with a twist.

Ingredients:

- 1 cup tortilla chips, crushed
- 1 cup black beans, cooked and mashed
- 1 cup vegan cheese sauce (nutritional yeast-based)
- 1/2 cup diced tomatoes
- 1/4 cup chopped green onions
- 1/4 cup sliced black olives
- 1/4 cup pickled jalapeños (adjust to spice preference)
- 1/4 cup vegan sour cream
- Salt and pepper to taste

Substitutions

- Customize with your favorite nacho toppings.
- Add avocado for extra creaminess.

Directions

1. In a pot, combine crushed tortilla chips, mashed black beans, vegan cheese sauce, diced tomatoes, chopped green onions, sliced black olives, pickled jalapeños, vegan sour cream, salt, and pepper.
2. Heat gently, stirring until heated through.
3. Enjoy the twist of this vegan breakfast nachos soup!

4 servings   330   35 min

Vegan Breakfast Bagel Soup

A breakfast bagel-inspired soup with a twist.

Ingredients:

- 2 whole wheat bagels, chopped
- 1 cup vegan cream cheese
- 1 cup cherry tomatoes, halved
- 1/2 cup red onion, thinly sliced
- 1/4 cup capers
- 1/4 cup chopped fresh dill
- Salt and pepper to taste

Directions

1. In a pot, combine chopped whole wheat bagels, vegan cream cheese, cherry tomatoes, red onion, capers, chopped fresh dill, salt, and pepper.
2. Heat gently, stirring until heated through.
3. Serve in bowls.
4. Enjoy the unique twist of this vegan breakfast bagel soup!

Substitutions

- Customize with your favorite bagel toppings.
- Add vegan lox for extra flavor.

4 servings | 340 | 50 min

Vegan Breakfast Samosa Soup

A savory and spiced breakfast samosa-inspired soup.

Ingredients:

- 2 cups diced potatoes
- 1 cup cooked chickpeas
- 1 onion, chopped
- 2 cloves garlic, minced
- 4 cups vegetable broth
- 1 cup chopped spinach
- 1 tsp curry powder
- 1/2 tsp ground turmeric
- Salt and pepper to taste

Directions

1. Sauté chopped onion and minced garlic until softened.
2. Add diced potatoes, cooked chickpeas, vegetable broth, chopped spinach, curry powder, ground turmeric, salt, and pepper.
3. Simmer for 20 minutes.
4. Enjoy the savory vegan breakfast samosa soup!

Substitutions

- Customize with your favorite spices and veggies.
- Top with vegan yogurt and cilantro.

4 servings

310

45 min

A fresh and veggie-packed breakfast spring rolls soup.

Vegan Breakfast Spring Rolls Soup

Ingredients:

- 8 spring roll wrappers, chopped
- 1 cup shredded carrots
- 1 cup cucumber, julienned
- 1 cup red bell pepper, thinly sliced
- 1 cup chopped fresh cilantro
- 1/4 cup chopped mint leaves
- 1/4 cup hoisin sauce
- 1/4 cup peanut sauce
- Lime wedges for garnish (optional)

Directions

1. In a pot, combine chopped spring roll wrappers, shredded carrots, julienned cucumber, thinly sliced red bell pepper, chopped fresh cilantro, chopped mint leaves, hoisin sauce, and peanut sauce.
2. Heat gently, stirring until heated through.
3. Serve in bowls.
4. Garnish with lime wedges if desired.
5. Enjoy the fresh vegan breakfast spring rolls soup!

Substitutions

- Customize with your favorite veggies and dipping sauces.
- Add tofu or tempeh for extra protein.

4 servings   350   40 min

Vegan Breakfast Empanadas Soup

A flavorful and pastry-inspired breakfast empanadas soup.

Ingredients:

- 4 vegan breakfast empanadas (store-bought or homemade)
- 1 cup salsa
- 4 cups vegetable broth
- 1/2 cup vegan cheese shreds
- 1/4 cup chopped fresh cilantro
- Lime wedges for garnish (optional)

Directions

1. In a pot, combine vegan breakfast empanadas, salsa, vegetable broth, vegan cheese shreds, and chopped fresh cilantro.
2. Heat gently, stirring until heated through.
3. Serve in bowls.
4. Garnish with lime wedges if desired.
5. Enjoy the flavorful vegan breakfast empanadas soup!

Substitutions

- Customize with your favorite empanadas flavors.
- Add avocado for extra creaminess.

We have a small favor to ask

Dear connoisseurs of soul-warming comfort and enthusiasts of plant-based goodness,

As we savor the final spoonfuls of warmth from our culinary journey through the pages of "Plant-Based Comfort Soups Cookbook: Soul-Warming Soups - Dive into 100+ Plant-Based Comfort Classics," I want to extend my heartfelt thanks for sharing in this comforting adventure with me. Together, we've explored the realm of soul-soothing soups, crafted with the goodness of plant-based ingredients.

Now, I come to you with a heartfelt request, one that holds profound significance for us —a small yet passionate publishing team. In the world of cookbooks, reviews are the secret ingredients that elevate a dish from merely good to truly exceptional. They are as elusive as the perfect balance of flavors in a comforting bowl of soup, yet they are the lifeblood of our creative spirit.

If these recipes have allowed you to experience the warmth and comfort of plant-based soups, filling your heart and belly with flavors that are both nourishing and soul-satisfying, I would be immensely grateful if you could spare a moment. Please return to the app or platform where you acquired this book, where you'll find a review button eagerly awaiting your input. A star rating and a brief sentence sharing your thoughts would be the culinary equivalent of a warm embrace in our world.

You see, as a small publisher, every review is a guiding light that illuminates our path. Your words have the power to inspire others to explore the world of plant-based comfort, all while celebrating the timeless appeal of comforting soups.

Rest assured, every review is not just welcomed but cherished. We understand that, like in any kitchen, even the most skilled chefs may occasionally make a minor mistake. If you happen to spot any such hiccup along the way, please understand that we've poured our hearts into this cookbook. We're human, and in the world of cooking, a touch of imperfection is part of the magic.

From the depths of my heart, thank you for choosing "Plant-Based Comfort Soups Cookbook," and thank you in advance for considering leaving a review. Your support fuels our passion for creating more delectable, plant-based, and soul-warming culinary experiences. Until we meet again in the pages of another cookbook, may your soups bring you solace, your flavors bring you joy, and your culinary journeys continue to nourish your body and spirit. To your health and culinary delight!

www.ingramcontent.com/pod-product-compliance
Lightning Source LLC
Chambersburg PA
CBHW080007180726

48002CB00021B/3135